Political Islam
in the
Global World

Political Islam
in the
Global World

Aini Linjakumpu

POLITICAL ISLAM IN THE GLOBAL WORLD

Published by
Ithaca Press
8 Southern Court
South Street
Reading
RG1 4QS
UK

Ithaca Press is an imprint of Garnet Publishing Limited

First Edition

ISBN-13: 978-0-86372-320-9

British Library Cataloguing-in-Publication Data
A catalogue record for this book is available from the British Library

Typeset by Samantha Barden
Jacket design by David Rose
Cover photo © iStockphoto.com/Nikontiger.
Photo shows a Muslim protest in London against Danish cartoons
depicting the Prophet Muhammad, 2006.

Printed by Biddles, UK

Contents

Preface   vii

List of abbreviations   xi

PART I

Introduction   3

PART II

1   The Euro-Mediterranean Co-operation: Participation and Legitimacy   27

2   The Muslim Brotherhood: Protest and Politics   59

3   The Internet: Myriad Voices and One Islam   97

PART III

4   The Concept and Strategies   129

Bibliography   149

Index   161

Preface

The connection of Islam and politics creates strong images and opinions. In the globalizing world, the political dimension of Islam is not decreasing – quite the contrary. During recent decades we have seen how Islam has generated political turbulence around the world. This has shown, at least, that the connection of Islam and politics is a very multidimensional and heterogeneous thing.

However, the many-sided character of political Islam is quite inadequately discussed in scientific research. Most methods of analysis used in assessing political Islam cannot take account of the multiple faces of this phenomenon, and do not necessarily even try to do so. This book attempts to develop an approach that allows the politicization of Islam in different circumstances and contexts to be examined. By doing this, one can look at the phenomenon of political Islam on many different levels. The point is not whether some phenomena is or is not about Islam, but to view *in what way and to what extent* some process is connected to Islam. The aim is to surpass the black-and-white dilemma where the politicization of Islam either exists or is totally absent.

Hence, this book concentrates on discussing *how Islam manifests itself politically*. The approach means that in the research of political Islam it is central to understand the ideas of politics and politicality. First, I will look at the political dimension of Islam through three case studies. Then I will examine different contexts and actors that influence how political Islam appears. Political Islam is approached through the possibilities offered by a theoretical frame of reference; the contents of Islam or its religious doctrine is thus not used in defining this phenomenon. The question, then, is *not how political dimensions manifest in Islam*.

Part I gives the background to Islam as a social phenomenon and research object. First, I will outline a constructive approach to Islam. This is done in order to challenge the religious-normative view on Islam. Second, I will review the study of religions and Islam on a general level, and I will present a critique of two branches of study of political Islam, which are opposite to the constructive approach. The critique is directed to the idea of over-politicization and to seeing Islam narrow-mindedly as a tool of politics.

Part I also presents the essential theoretical tools I have used in this work. The main concepts are politics and identity. By deconstructing the idea of politics I will construct for this book a meaningful view on what is the nature of politics, where it takes place and the role of different actors. In this book, politics is interpreted as a conflictual and aspectual phenomenon, which is conveyed to people through linguistic expressions. The focus point is to find how something becomes political – that is, how it politicizes.

The second central concept is political identity. Examining identity helps us to understand more accurately the logic of actions through the self-understanding of political actors, and the meaning of self–other relationships. The importance of identity in studying political Islam is very essential because the political dimension of Islam is often connected to identity, and to the formation and existence of a community.

Politicization and study of identity are, by their nature, attached to language. This means that texts especially carry "traces" of the research object. Something exists through language and by giving a meaning to it, which allows connections to other things. In this context I will apply the idea of articulation and I will suggest that the conflictual nature of politics and the existence of contradictions get their linguistic form in the process of articulation.

The end of Part I gives a more precise frame of study and also introduces empirical case studies. These case studies are more fully examined in Part II. The first relates to the co-operation between the European Union (EU) and the non-EU Mediterranean countries – that is, the Euro-Mediterranean Co-operation. In this part, the Barcelona process, which started at the end of 1995, will be examined more thoroughly. The role of Islam has not been central in this process but certain elements of co-operation – the discussions on terrorism and the clash of civilizations – imply a direct reference to Islam and its role in both international and national contexts.

The second case deals with one of the oldest and most well-known active political Muslim movements, the Muslim Brotherhood of Egypt. This movement can be regarded as a typical form of political Islam. Even now, the relationship between Islam and politics inside the Brotherhood demands being questioned: in what way does Islam actually show in the ideology of the Muslim Brotherhood? In this context, the role of the state of Egypt in the formation of opposition politics is a central theme.

In the third case, the idea of politicization of Islam is taken to a more abstract level. The focus here is on the discussion groups on the Internet. There are diverse and rich conversations on Islam and related topics on the Internet, and there we can see most clearly how heterogeneous the political dimension of Islam really is. With the Internet we can examine new possibilities for global action and communality. One example, discussed in this book, is the idea of virtual umma.

The final part of this book suggests as a summary a definition of political Islam on the basis of the theoretical and methodological tools used in analyzing these empirical cases. Furthermore, new approaches to each case study will enlarge the perspective when focusing on the politicization of Islam. The idea is to analyze the *strategies of political Islam* in a global world.

Aini Linjakumpa

Abbreviations

ARI	alt.religion.islam (Internet discussion group)
CFSP	Common Foreign and Security Policy
CMC	computer-mediated communication
EU	European Union
GMP	Global Mediterranean Policy
HDZ	Hrvatska demokratska zajednica (Croatian Democratic Union)
HSLS	Hrvatska socijalno-liberalna stranta (Croatian Social Liberal Party)
IRC	Internet Relay Chat
MUD	Multi-User Domain
NATO	North Atlantic Treaty Organization
NDP	National Democratic Party
NGO	non-governmental organizations
OIC	Organization of Islamic Conference
SEM countries	southern and eastern Mediterranean countries
SRI	soc.religion.islam (Internet discussion group)
UN	United Nations

PART I

Introduction

A constructive approach to Islam

In many ways, the study of religions is exceptional not least because it involves a strong element of personal experiences. Moreover, this experiental content is very difficult to translate into the language of science. For a religious person, religion is something sacrosanct and unchangeable. There are also views that religion is about deeper values and basic questions of life that science is unable to answer, even in principle (Ketola 1997, 12).

The perspectives of science and religion are necessarily different but they do not need to be mutually exclusive since they have very different starting points and objectives. Therefore, the religious views of a religious person and the religious views of a scholar are two different things. They signify for each person different things in relation to religion. For a believer, important things are, for example, a personal relationship with God or salvation.

In interpreting Islam the conceptions of a believer are based on religious information, and the conceptions of a scholar on scientific knowledge. Relying on scientific knowledge means that the religion under scrutiny is seen as a social phenomenon, something that has taken shape in the actions of human beings. In that case, one studies human beings who are in contact with religion, not the religion itself.

The difference in religious and scientific knowledge also implicates a different approach to a religiously defined reality. One can speak of social and normative reality and interaction between these two. The basic assumption of this book is a conception of a socially constructed reality where things are formed through meanings and have no essentialist nature. In relation to Islam, this means that one cannot give any timeless, self-evident or unchangeable interpretation. Socially constructed reality, though, has a strong interaction with the religious reality defined by normative dimension.

Normativeness is evaluation of truth or acceptability of religious expressions and actions (Ketola 1997, 23). Emphasizing normativeness implies that Islam is interpreted through religious doctrines, and the heterogeneous totality of Islam appears to be more one-sided when seen through a narrow religious belief system. In that case there is a monolithic view on Islam that does not take into account the implications of social reality to the formation of a norm system and religious doctrines, for example. According to a constructive approach, social structures are constantly changing and renewing, and socialization takes place in different interactive relations. Structures and social relationships are not predestined and they are not conveyed to everyone in the same way.

The constructive interpretation of Islam affects, on the one hand, the interpretation of the *birth* of Islam, and on the other, how *contemporary* Islam is seen. According to normative Islam, the birth of Islam appears through unquestionable doctrines. This applies also to the basic sources of Islam: the Quran, *hadiths* and *sunna*. The birth of the Quran is understood, in the orthodox sense, so that the Quran is given from the heavens to the Prophet Mohammed as a complete work. This interpretation demonstrates how the Quran in a believer's mind is actually the word of God, which is flawless from the beginning. The task of the Prophet is only to receive the "word" and convey it to people. (Räisänen 1986, 123)

The constructive view challenges this way of thinking, and thus the origin of Islam must be interpreted in a different way. The birth of Islam and its origins can be seen as a *process*, not as a thing originating from a sudden divine message. The constructive view emphasizes that the birth of the Quran is closely attached to social and historical events. The revelations, on which the Quran is based, came to Mohammed over a long time period, and the formation of the actual text took even longer. Mohammed received the revelations in an auditory form and transmitted them forward in an oral form. Oral communication continued even after the first texts were written down.

The canonization of the Quran – i.e. the process during which the Quran took its present form – lasted long after the death of Mohammed. There were several versions of the Quran, and gradually one of those was accepted as an official version and the others lost "the battle". The actual process was very multifaceted and political; constructing the authentic version caused some debate among the Muslim community: which parts should be taken into the Holy Book and which not (Räisänen 1986, 17–19). This process is not about how to create as authentic a written construction of God's will as possible; rather, the question is how pure orthodoxy was formed.

The impact of the social processes is strongly attached to the *interpretation* of Islam, and thereby to the relationship between normative Islam and social reality. The interpretation of Islam constitutes an essential part of the totality in which the internal relationships of Islam and power relations are determined. The interpretation itself defines how the normative aspects of religion are formed in social reality – i.e. how religious doctrine becomes practice. Therefore, the interpretation is the element in between the spiritual and the secular, and typically it is seen in the form of Islamic law (*sharia*).

According to traditional Islamic doctrine, the interpretation of Islam takes place in conformity with the four basic principles. These are the Quran, the manners of the Prophet (*sunna* and *hadith*), analogic reasoning (*qyias*), and the consensus of the learned ones (*ijma*). Since the early days of Islam, the three latter have been the methods or techniques of "finding" and defending the law, which contains a lot of conformity. The Quran, on the other hand, is seen as an unchanging and ageless text (Rosen 1989, 42).

In Sunni Islam, there are four main schools of thought (Hanafi, Maliki, Shafii and Hanbali) in the sphere of which Islam has been interpreted throughout history. The possibility of interpretation is, in principle, an open choice because in Islam there are no clergy, for example, between God and people, as in Christianity. There is, however, a religious elite, *ulama*, in Sunni Islam that resembles Christian clergy. *Ulama* consists of persons with a legal education (Esposito 1988, 174). Historically the meaning of a religious elite has been significant because it has had the power to define the content of Islam and has been the mediator of the religious message to lay persons. As John Esposito remarks, the religious leaders became the lawyers, theologians and teachers of the Muslim community, which interpreted and guarded Islamic law and tradition (Esposito 1988, 59).

The ways of interpreting Islam have varied according to the times. There have been periods when interpretation was progressive and renewing, and when it has searched new possibilities in a new social context. The early days of Islam were a vigorous time of doctrine creation, and the main body of the doctrines of Islam took shape at that time. On the other hand, there have been periods when the interpretation of Islamic law has followed existing paths and when the question of creating a new doctrine was seen as less important or not permitted. This kind of period extended roughly from the 10th to the 18th centuries. That phase has been called "closing the gates of *ijtihad*", the phrase illustrating the idea of standstill. The situation changed somewhat from the beginning of the 18th century when there were new pressures against the doctrine of Islam. These were, among others, the challenges of Western colonialism and modernization in many Islamic countries (see e.g. Ayubi 1991, 56–57 and Esposito 1987, 19).

The process during which the holy text gets its inner meaning is declared as *authentic* (Arkoun 1994, 33). The birth and upkeep of authenticity is, by its nature, attached to power and politics. In defining authenticity one gives influence to social processes and through them to people's lives. Guarding the orthodoxy is to exercise power, in which one can resort to the norm of authenticity. Many phenomena of political Islam are based on this: who can define orthodoxy and what does it means when you attack it? It can be seen that different Muslim groups strive for orthodoxy and authenticity but, alternatively, they also attack the concepts of orthodoxy of other actors.

Understanding orthodoxy and authenticity is important because they are the forces that direct and generate the actions of Muslim activists. To these activists, it is significant how the orthodoxy is defined in different situations. For the scholar, however, it is essential to see the constructive nature of orthodoxy. In other words, orthodoxy is not a constant state, though every interpreter of orthodoxy would like to be the sole authority.

The over-politicization of Islam and Islam as an instrument of politics

Seeing the differences of language and reality between science and religion, and between a scholar and a believer, is the basis for studying religion. Furthermore, one must take notice of the differences of various fields of science and social levels. Islam can be understood, for example, as a religious, cultural or political phenomenon. The same event, act or state of affairs – e.g. a Muslim banking system or the veiling of Muslim women – can be interpreted simultaneously from the point of view of religious science, sociology or political science (cf. Ketola 1997, 21). The special questions and basic principles of different fields of science define largely what will be studied and what kind of answers are possible.

When taking account of the heterogeneousness of different approaches, it is important to realize that the study of religion is in itself an interdisciplinary activity. Studying Islam with the methodology of cultural science also enables the study of political implications of Islam and vice versa. The view of political science cannot ignore the cultural meanings of Islam – though in that case questions arise from political science.

The politically oriented study of Islam since the 1960s is characterized by its connection to general world politics and especially to the political events in the Middle East. Therefore, the importance of the Arab–Muslim world has been emphasized in Western Islamic studies. This geographical area has become significant because of its political and strategic value. The United States of America and Europe have been dependent on the natural resources of this area, mainly on oil. In the 1970s this dependency meant that the oil crisis caused grave problems. Another factor affecting Islamic studies is the state of Israel and its relations with Palestine and the rest of the Arab–Muslim world. Since the founding of Israel, in 1948, conflicts and crises have been numerous.

Though aforementioned factors and other events that have molded the reality of the Middle East are not "directly" connected to Islam, the growing importance of this area has meant that interest towards Islam has also risen. Through different events, the consciousness of the existence of this area and its problems has widened the horizon of research into relating themes. The Western Islamic discussion has, especially in the aftermath of the Cold War, gained new nuances in which Islam is seen as a threat. This image has not been diminished by events connected to Muslim terrorism in the Muslim states around the Mediterranean.

There are many different approaches to political Islam and therefore it is not possible, and not even necessary, to do a broad general introduction of the studies concerning Islamic politics. Therefore I shall construe two relevant ways to carry out Islam studies in political science, and my own approach will be critical towards them. The first of those two ways is connected to *over-politicization of Islam* when interpreting political events in Muslim countries, and in the second Islam is seen as a *tool* of politics.

Over-politicization of Islam

In studying the politics of Muslim countries, Islam is often over-emphasized in relation to other social phenomena and, furthermore, is seen as having straightforward implications for politics. Islam is interpreted as an essentially political phenomenon, which means the relationship between Islam and politics, or social life as a whole, is seen, for example, in the following way:

> Islam is not just a religious order. It is a complete way of life for the individual, the society, the state, and the nation. Islam does not recognize national, racial, or linguistic boundaries; it is a universal doctrine that does not permit a separation between the secular and the religious. [...] [A]ll human action and interaction within the Muslim community is by definition regulated by Islam (Ismael and Ismael 1991, 44).

In this passage Islam is seen as a universal system in which different areas of human life are united. This is monotheism (*tawhid*), where there is only one God and His will and commandments are overarching: they cover all creatures and every area of life. So, *tawhid* does not just mean that there is only one God, it also means the oneness of God's will which is targeted both to an individual Muslim and the whole Muslim community. Therefore religion belongs to every area of life: political, social and moral (Esposito 1987, 39; Esposito 1988, 26).

In this normative-classic interpretation of Islam, the relationship between Islam and politics is understood as unambiguous. An individual must follow God's teachings in all areas of life. Hence, politics is also something that belongs to religious affairs. In studying Islam, the problematic nature of normative Islam is particularly underlined when Muslims themselves are studying Islam. If the study is taking place inside the normative system, religion may be approached from a theological point of view, and in that case reality outside of religion may be hard to interpret (cf. Waarderburg 1978, 338).

However, a normative approach to studying Islam is not used by (convinced) Muslims alone. Many non-Muslims also interpret Islam and its sociopolitical implications by that method. A traditional oriental approach particularly sees Islam in an ideal light: society is a product of religion – i.e. it is organized according to divine will (Barakat 1993, 119). One example of the oriental approach is Esposito's view on Islam:

[R]eligion is not separate but rather integral to every aspect of life: prayer, fasting, politics, law, and society. This belief is reflected not only in the doctrine of *tawhid* but also, quite concretely, in the development of the Islamic state and Islamic law (the *shariah*) (Esposito 1983, 4).

The over-politicization of Islam also implicates over-Islamization of Muslim communities. This creates two intertwined problems. First, it disregards the history of Islam and the problems it entails. Second, Islam is abstracted in a way that bypasses those forms of it that are created in social contexts. Though the religious and political government was in the hands of one man, and therefore it can be said that there was earthly and spiritual unity in governing the community, it is historically difficult to perceive the unity of these spheres as a fact. After the death of Mohammed, the caliph succeeded him as the leader of the community and he was, as his predecessor, a religious and political leader (see e.g. Piscatori 1988, 11 and Ayubi 1991, 2–18).

However, explaining the political side of Islam by religious sources and appealing to the history of Islam is not totally justified. Eickelman and Piscatori emphasize that politics and religion were separated soon after the death of the Prophet. This separation was connected to the emergence of dynasties (Eickelman and Piscatori 1996, 46). On the other hand, Aziz Ayubi claims that the Quran and *hadith* do not specify how the government should be organized or what it should look like. According to Ayubi, Islam had not so much defined the nature of the historical Muslim state but this form of governance has influenced Islamic tradition (Ayubi 1991, 120).

If the relationship between Islam and all spheres of society, especially politics, is seen as inseparable, then, in principle, everything is political in Muslim societies. But this view disregards the political culture of these states, which could have been influenced quite strongly, for example, by Western political culture. As in every political community, sociopolitical structures are clearly visible in Muslim communities, though they could be overlapping with the religious ones (see Eickelman and Piscatori 1996, 56–57).

The link between Islam and politics cannot be seen as inevitable, though it may be quite important in some cases. However, the idea of over-politicization means an undeniable bond between these two areas and thus Islam would be political by nature. This book looks at this inevitable connection and also gives a different perspective in studying the relationship between politics and Islam.

Islam as an instrument of politics

The over-politicization of Islam indicates that Islam is seen as being capable of influencing decisively both the form and content of politics. This view is challenged by interpretations according to which Islam is significant in politics only in an indirect and instrumental way. Consequently, Islam is involved in politics in order to gain something with it, mainly non-religious objectives. Islam is taken advantage of, and there are no "genuine" Muslim politics. Religion is used by politics: "[I]n evaluating the political importance of religions and the religious side of some political phenomenon, one must concentrate on *the political use of religions*" (Melasuo 1991b, 43; italics in original).

Religions, therefore, are "directly or indirectly at least a part of that political ideology and even the political system whose relation to religion is partly defined by the fact of how religion is used in politics" (ibid.). When religion is "used" in politics, there arises the question of legitimacy and control. Religion is a tool with which one can sell his/her own politics – in other words, justify political actions and political control (Barakat 1993, 129–30). Ayubi emphasizes the relationship between state and Islam when he analyzes how Islam has taken over the state: "There was indeed a connection between religion and politics throughout much of the history of the Islamic State, but this was the outcome of the State taking over religion as a legitimizing shield for its activity" (Ayubi 1991, 120). The argument refers especially to the actions of the elite. In a broader sense, other groups can use religion in politics as well as, for example, different Muslim movements.

Instrumental interpretation of religion basically emphasizes separation of different spheres of life. Religion is assumed to be something that is taken into politics in certain situations. Politics transform with the situation but religion is merely used in practicing politics; it has nothing to do with these practices. Phenomena are examined according to whether they are "genuinely" Islamic or not. This contains, implicitly, a supposition of "genuine" Islamic policy: "When we think of the Gulf War from the Islamic point of view, we can see that there is nothing Islamic in it" (Melasuo 1991a, 22).

[10]

When Islam is interpreted as a tool of politics, then it doesn't seem possible that it could form an ideological or symbolic basis for practicing politics. The actors are seen as having a utilitarian viewpoint; they need something with the help of religion, even if that something doesn't have any real connection to religion. This interpretation does not accept that religion could be political in itself, or that there could be religiously motivated or justified politics.

Both of these two interpretations have some explanatory force and they hold true in some cases. Regardless of this, neither can be valued as a meaningful general starting point. The over-politicization of Islam – the inevitable bond between Islam and politics – means endless reductional thinking where everything is connected to everything. Then, it is hard to interpret individual cases from the political point of view because politics is inbuilt into everything. The problem here is too broad a conception of politics, which has therefore lost its explanatory power.

The "instrumental Islam" idea does not, on the other hand, see a "natural" possibility to link Islam and politics. Religion and politics are separate sectors. Islam does not have a political aspect; it is only used and abused in politics. In this case, *politics is understood too narrowly*; it belongs expressly to state activity and to the political life around it.

Research of politics in studying Islam

The common problem of the aforementioned approaches is in their weak conceptions of politics. Besides that, these approaches are temporally and locally abstract, which underlines their Islamic foundation. Understanding the idea and content of politics is important when one wants to understand the political dimensions of Islam. Thus, theorizing politics opens a route to examining the political side of Islam. This is why the starting point of this book is to clarify the concept of politics.

The traditional concept of politics emphasizes representational politics where politicians (*actors of politics*) are practicing politics inside or/and through institutions (*location of politics*) in order to reach their objectives (*idea of politics*). In analyzing the relationship between Islam and politics or the politicization of Islam, this kind of conception of politics has quite limited power to explain or interpret events. When I talk about politics, I do not refer to these kinds of practices or structures. With regards to political Islam it would not give a wide enough approach because many phenomena I have dealt with would remain outside its scope and even outside this definition of politics. Therefore, the new "wave" of political Islam could not be interpreted because it simply would not fit this definition. An important part of political Islam can thus be found outside the traditional conception of politics.

In this book, I will adapt the so-called *aspectual concept of politics*, which emphasizes that the *existence of contradictions* illustrates the *substance of politics*. Here it is important to think about the origins of politics – i.e. how things enter the field of politics or how they are made political. The conflictual nature is not, in this definition, a disturbing factor in politics; more, it defines the uniqueness of politics and separates it from other social phenomena – e.g. culture, religion or economy. The word "conflict" is often connected to concrete action – e.g. armed confrontation. But here conflict is defined more loosely. Conflict refers to the opposition of political actors or participants in relation to the objectives of politics or each other (Palonen 1979, 84). The conflicting perspective of politics does not presume that there is actual opposition. However, "any action – in order to be consciously political – must be prepared to encounter resistance" (Palonen 1993, 100).

Along with the conflictual dimension there is another way to unravel the traditional concept of politics, namely to consider *the location of politics*: "where" politics is situated. According to traditional thinking, politics is a separate sector, area or field that can clearly be defined into one separate entity. It is a single sector of life similar to economy or culture. This kind of *sectoral view on politics* embodies an idea of autonomy in different areas of life. In order to be politics, the research object must be situated in the sector of politics (Palonen 1979, 24–25). This sector may consist of smaller subsectors – e.g. financial policy or foreign policy. In this concept, politics is explicitly situated inside the representational system. Thus, parties and their supporters are an essential part of the political system.

The concept of politics that is applied in this study is not attached to any particular institutions or sectors but to the idea of politics, to the conflictive side of it. This concept, as distinct from sectoral policy, has been called *aspect politics*: "[E]very phenomena has or can have a political aspect though they do not necessarily have a political aspect; therefore no phenomena is not 'shielded' against politicization" (Palonen 1988a, 19).

This definition means that politics is not a separate part of reality; rather, it is a *view* on reality. Phenomena of social life "cannot be divided into politics and non-politics; the same phenomenon can include both political and non-political aspects" (Palonen 1979, 26). Discovering politics and politicization requires *"reading"*, through which politics is interpreted. Politics must be found among other phenomena because it does not exist objectively or in any pure form in a certain place. Thus, the results of political research are *interpretations*, not so much unequivocal truths (Palonen 1993, 12–13; Palonen 1988a, 19 and Palonen 1988b, 99, 108).

Actualization of the political aspect means that something *becomes political*. Making something political is "an interpretative operation that changes something that is considered non-political to political or an operation that increases politicization of that phenomenon" (Palonen 1993, 91). The aspectual view on politics is directing research in many ways. First of all, the presence of certain political aspects does not eliminate other aspects of the same phenomenon; it only excludes them when concentrating on the political side. Other aspects do not necessarily need examination unless they are used in political evaluation. There is no need to examine thoroughly the whole phenomenon. Second, concentrating on the political aspect of a certain area of a phenomena does not necessitate that politicization would be a decisive factor in that area. Third, the guiding principle is that there is no predetermined rule in which politicization may be found (Palonen 1993, 14).

In the sectoral research of politics, Islam is either a totally non-political or sectorally "religious-political" phenomenon. From the point of view of aspectual politics, Islam can, on the other hand, be interpreted in some cases to belong to the political field: thus it is a *potentially* political phenomenon. On the other hand, in a more limited sense, political expressions of Islam can be found in places where they were perhaps not expected to be found. Therefore, the possibility of finding political expressions from other than accustomed places (in Islam, for example Muslim states or political Muslim movements) is guided, in this book, by the selection of empirical cases and their interpretation. Thus, part of the purpose of this book is to find new expressions of political Islam and "reread" the traditional ways of political practices in Islam.

The definition of aspectual politics provides the possibility of constructing politicization according to the situation or context. In relation to Islam, this means that Islam does not automatically become political in every possible circumstance, even if one *could* find possibilities in different forms of politics. The Islamic tendency of politics (or the generally religious and cultural tendency) does not, in any case, extend to every phenomena. The politicization of Islam is only possible in some cases. In addition to this, politicization of Islam must be interpreted because it may have quite diverse forms in different cases and contexts.

In defining politics, the third crucial element is political actors: who practices politics? A conventional view suggests that politicians are the primary actors in politics. Politicians are voters' representatives and voters have given them the license to act in politics. Politicians are the conveyors of politics.

Defining aspectual politics means that politics is situated more freely in various structures and phenomena of society. In the sense of aspectual politics one cannot interpret that there would be politicians on the one hand and participants in politics on the other. Potentially, anyone can be a political actor. For this reason, a political agenda is not determined solely by politicians but everyone is a potential actor in politics, i.e. a politician.

When we discuss political actors, we also consider the idea of political space. Essential in this space is how different participants have the possibility to act and articulate their own interests. Political space is controlled by those who have the power to define political questions in a certain context. Whose definitions has relevance in a certain context? Who can influence the existence or change the contents of political space? If a political actor is capable of articulating his or her own interests through specific themes in certain places, s/he can create his/her own political space and influence on the form of existing political spaces.

The articulation of politics and political language

When political space is formed – i.e. the conflictual side – and contradictions of politics become present, they are expressed in *linguistic forms*. Politics is not, thus, something straightforward; it is created by language and by giving a meaning. Through language and meaning, connections can then be made to other things and structures. With this in mind, I will apply the idea of *articulation* and suggest that the *conflictual nature of politics and the existence of contradictions get their linguistic form in the process of articulation.*

With regards articulation, things are both *clearly stated* and *connected to each other* (see Hall 1992a, 368). Both definitions are necessary if one wants to study the manifestation of politics from linguistic expressions. It must be understood, too, that meanings are interconnected.

Stating clearly means expressing and introducing both differences and similarities. In this process something is taken up so that it becomes existent: linguistic forms enable the articulation of things. If something that is to be articulated could conceptually exist and be outlined, it should have boundaries around it and must be defined in relation to other things and objects.

Naming is one part of stating clearly. Giving a name is the "choice of an individual or a group in a situation where there is more than one option" (Pekonen 1993, 10–13). When something is named, it is defined and given borders. Calling something by name is a symbolic process where that thing is created in a certain way. Because of this, the referent (the thing being referred to) is not a cultural constant; a language produces and rewrites it.

Political objectives can be expressed through articulation – i.e. one can name those aspirations that are the goals of political activity. Political goals cannot be seen as objective targets that could concretely be reached. Rather, the objectives are metaphors and symbols with which concrete policy is produced. This indicates that one must emphasize caution in interpreting Muslim politics because certain tendencies – such as forming a Muslim state – should be seen metaphorically, not as absolute and as the sole content of politics.

In the process of articulation, which takes place in various social practices, bonds of meaning are born between different things, concepts, actions and phenomena (Laclau and Mouffe 1985, 105). This is close to the other aspect of articulation, which connects together different elements and things. Grossberg's definition of articulation clarifies this:

> Articulation: coupling, analyzing: a practice where things that do not necessarily have any previous mutual relation are coupled together; theoretical and historical practice with which is produced a certain structure of relations that define a certain society (Grossberg 1995, 268–269).

In articulation one describes the relations of practices and their implications and how these practices may have different, often unpredictable, effects (Grossberg 1995, 209). Practices are transferred from one context to another and at the same time connections are constructed between things:

> Articulation is producing identity with the peak of difference, producing unity from fragments, producing structure from practices. Articulation couples this practice to that impact, this text to that meaning, this meaning to that reality, this experience to that reality, this experience to that politics. These connections can themselves be articulated as a part of larger structures (Grossberg 1995, 20).

In the process of articulation, different practices can be thought to appear together, even if they are very dissimilar, but they are not necessarily attached to each other (Hall 1992a, 82). By this, one can avoid reductional thinking (Hall 1992a, 369) that shows, for example, in the idea of over-politicization of Islam (which I criticized earlier) where the relationship between Islam and politics is seen as something inevitable and natural.

In this context, I am interested especially in political articulation: how things relate to each other in a conflictual way. One must notice, however, that articulation can also be non-political. In this case, different things are connected and seen as parts of a whole in a way that does not create conflictual juxtaposition between participants.

From various articulations a totality of practices will emerge in certain contexts, and then something can be defined (in this case "Islam" or "political Islam"). The diversity of articulation means inevitably that emerging structures take a very different form in different situations and contexts. And, as previously was stated, the articulation of Islam may also be non-political when it does not cause any conflict between different participants.

In studying political Islam, the concept of articulation directs research to those processes where Islam is the basis for political differences. Then, political differences and causes of conflict are articulated through linguistic processes linked to Islam. The idea of articulation enables the existent and predetermined significative relation between Islam and politics to be dissolved. Islam can be seen as a whole that is articulated in various ways, and political articulation is only one possibility among others. Uniting Islam and politics has its historical foundation, but here the aim is first to unravel the relationship between Islam and politics, and second to rearticulate it. Islam can be understood as a social potential that can be articulated politically in numerous ways and in various intensities.

Political identities and Islam

It is possible to understand political Islam better by considering the meaning of identity. Particularly since the Cold War, the debate about identity has been lively because it is thought to have a specific role in generating conflicts. People's self-understanding and identity have thus become increasingly essential in directing political research and practices. The identity question is part of a discussion of politicization of cultures; one example of this is Samuel Huntington's idea of the clash of civilizations. The assumed change of the role of the nation state has also affected the development of non-national, local and global identities, and their growing importance (see e.g. Cerny 1996, 629; Hunter 1995, 42 and Laclau 1994, 1).

With regards "identity" I mean the understanding that gives identifiable characteristics to an individual or group. Through identity one can understand what kind of person one really is. In order to understand oneself there must exist an outside party, an otherness. Later, this book looks at political identities which differ, in my view, from, for instance, cultural identities. In talking about identities one must also take account of the difference between individual and collective identities.

Individual identity is linked to a person's understanding of him or herself, and identity is therefore closely connected to the person and personality of that individual. This kind of thinking is close to behavioral research (cf. e.g. Mokros 1996, 4–5) and psychology. In collective identity, self-understanding is linked to community: how an individual understands that he or she is part of a bigger structure. Therefore, we can speak of the self-understanding of a community.

Collective identity refers to human beings' commitment to the collective, i.e. to the group s/he belongs to and identifies with. The idea of collective identity is closely connected to the formation of a community; identity obtains its concrete form through communities. Those communities are upheld by this feeling of togetherness. Also the space where the community exists and is active belongs to the idea of community.

Additionally, the community needs some kind of social system that makes the members of the community act in a way that is meaningful to the community as a whole. Community is based on a communal sense that can manifest in actions or feelings. Then it is possible to speak of functional or symbolic communities (see Lehtonen 1990, 23–28 and Jones 1995, 21).

In modern times, forms of collective identity are often linked to people or nations, and particularly to how they have tried to understand their own identity alongside, and relationship with, other nations (cf. Goldstein and Rayner 1994, 372). Benedict Anderson has examined how nationalistic identities are formed. He talks about imagined political communities when he defines the idea of people. According to him, community is imagined because even the representatives of the smallest nations do not know their fellow citizens. In their mind, however, lies an image of communality. In Anderson's view, communities are imagined almost without exception – even those that are based on close contacts. There is no concrete bind between the members of a community but still they have a conception that they somehow do have a connection with people like them (Anderson 1991, 6).

In Islam, the idea of community is specially linked to *umma*, which is the concept of Muslim community. Historically, *umma* has had various forms. At some times, the religious aspect has been the priority; at other times, it's been the sociopolitical aspects. Regardless of the definition of *umma*, it has in any case been the central concept in understanding the basis of collective action from the Islamic point of view (see Ayubi 1991, 18). According to John Esposito, *umma* is the tool of God's will, and the Prophet Mohammed particularly, along with his contemporary community, are an example for communities and collective actions after him (see Esposito 1987, 2 and Esposito 1988, 37).

Politicization of identity

What makes identity become political? The crucial factor is the questions concerning differences and differentiating. As explained earlier, things and phenomena do not appear directly to us, but through the linguistic world. The same holds true with identities. Adapting the idea of articulation constructed earlier, when identity becomes political the relation between self and other is articulated – i.e. produced as a phenomenon and combined as a whole in the form of different linguistic expressions – so that there arises a conflictual situation between the bearers of identity.

From this definition we can see that politics and identity are fundamentally intertwined concepts. If politicization generally means the conflictual articulation of things, then identity is attached to actors, i.e. to those whose articulations are in conflict. In that case, the focus is on the politicization of the actors' identities: when an actor politicizes something, it happens in relation to some other actor, be it an individual or a collective. Political identity is, thus, the conflictual articulation of self and other.

Politicization does not belong just to the contents of some phenomenon but at the same time to the conditions of the existence of actors. Through identities, and by politicizing them, we are able to examine those implications of politicization that define the self-understanding of political actors and their relation to other participants. The concepts of politics and identity are not, then, separate but complementary.

Identity is based on communality and, in the same vein, to dissimilarity; identity is dependent on this. There is no identity *per se*. It grows from different relations where *otherness is an essential and inevitable part of self.* Interaction is a condition for mutual existence of the self and others. Thus, the existence and construction of otherness is not just about negative things. As Lois McNay mentions, the politics of differences should be seen as a possibility, not as something to get rid of in order to achieve political unity (McNay 1992, 110). One must keep in mind, though, that this inevitability (and positivity) of interaction does not wipe out the possible negative aspects that belong to a self–other construction. In a negative sense, otherness and unlikeness are close to the ideas of exclusion and marginalization.

The content of otherness is connected to the heterogeneity of social contexts and of the power relations that construct identity. This means that if we want to analyze Islamic identity and politics, we must understand otherness as a contextual element, not as a setting that never changes. For example, it is obvious that, for some Egyptian Muslim groups, otherness is a different concept than for some Muslim communities in France.

Defining the concepts of self and other brings politicization closer to the actual political processes. The politics of difference is that aspect which determines the subject's position in a situation: What am I in relation to other? Defining oneself means consciousness of oneself, how one understands one's own existence: Who am I? Who am I not? To see the differences between self and other there must be sources of identity that make your own existence unique. Politicizing oneself goes through the conflict with otherness and through articulating differences.

From this we can deduce that politicizing Islamic identity also needs otherness for its counterpart. Islamic identity is not political in itself but in certain situations it can articulate itself in a political way. Generally, Islam is a most interesting theme in relation to politicizing identity. Traditional religious doctrines offer a stable and natural base for constructing identity because they stress the idea of a common Muslim community for all Muslims, i.e. *umma*, and separating oneself from others.

In building Islamic identity it is significant to justify political existence so that it would touch on a personal and collective level all the potential political followers, and also enable the division of people into political friends and enemies. According to Islamic tradition, the division between self and other follows roughly the division between *dar-al-islam* and *dar-al-harb*. *Dar-al-islam* literally means "the house of Islam". It refers to the area where Muslims and Islamic law dominate. *Dar-al-harb* is "the house of war", which basically includes the rest of the world.

Normally, this division is understood so that otherness is concretely outside of Muslim areas (e.g. the West or different sides of Western lifestyle). However, otherness is not just something outside of the community; it can also be detected inside it. The internal otherness of the community is, for example, a secularized way of life and things forbidden by religion, which in the longer term cause internal decay in the community. This division between *dar-al-islam* and *dar-al-harb* is, of course, strongly simplified; it has mainly heuristic value and is based on a normative interpretation of Islam. As one can see from the empirical cases in this study, Islamic identities construct in very diverse ways.

Introduction to case studies

At the beginning of this book I suggested that the typical problem in examining the phenomenon of political Islam has been that theories and approaches have concentrated only on some aspects of that phenomenon.

Furthermore, some approaches have tried to be too all-embracing, and thus all contextual elements of the phenomenon have not been taken into account.

Criticism was especially targeted at two particular approaches: over-politicization, and using Islam as a tool. The problem in the first approach is in seeing the relationship of Islam and politics as being too inevitable and natural. It is a reductionist way of interpreting the political aspect of Islam. With regards using Islam as a tool, there was no apparent natural connection between Islam and politics. Islam is politically significant only if "politicians" utilize it. In this approach the spheres of politics and religion are seen as separate spaces which behave according to their own logic.

With these approaches we can only deal with a part of political Islam. As an alternative to them, I have tried to construct a theoretical approach with which it is possible to study very different cases that illuminate the political possibilities of Islam. Central theoretical tools in my approach are the concepts of politics and identity. These concepts are closely connected to language, and here I have used the idea of articulation: the conflictual nature of politics and the existence of contradictions obtain their linguistic forms in the process of articulation.

With regards identities, I have suggested that when identities become political the relationship between the self and other is articulated – i.e. it is produced as a phenomenon and is united to one whole in the form of different linguistic expressions. Thus, the bearers of identity are those political actors who are influenced by articulation, and political identity means the conflictual articulation of self and other.

All in all, this approach means that the phenomenon is being approached by constructing a theory of politics. An applied concept of politics and the idea of articulation basically emphasize a contextual interpretation where the actors and situations to be observed are not predetermined. That is why the selection of empirical cases can be relatively free because the primary motive of research is to examine how Islam is articulated in each particular case. So, my preliminary idea of political Islam is a form of Islam that is articulated in a conflictual way.

This book considers three empirical cases: the Euro-Mediterranean Co-operation, the Muslim Brotherhood of Egypt and Islam debates on the Internet.

These cases are not necessarily determined through Islam, i.e. they are not presumed primarily to illustrate Islam. The only precondition is that Islam in a political sense is likely to be involved. The purpose of this study is to interpret *how* the political articulations of Islam are constructed in each case. It is easy to find differences in these cases, e.g. in the *level of official involvement, the level of actorness* and *the nature of the community.*

For example, when we talk about the articulation of Islam, the state is still an essential partner in the power relation. The Euro-Mediterranean Co-operation represents a clearly official context in which international politics is being practiced. The Muslim Brotherhood acts as a semi-official political actor inside the political context of Egypt. The Internet discussion groups are, for their part, unofficial and informal forums.

The difference in the levels of actorness is clearly shown in these cases. There are actors on an individual level, and there are smaller and larger collectives. Collectives are the international-level actors in the Euro-Mediterranean Co-operation; they act at governmental level and consist mainly of representatives of various governments. The Muslim Brotherhood is a different kind of collective. In addition, we can also talk of individual actors on the Internet who act on a global level.

There are several kinds of contexts, and therefore actors are different in each case. Their role in the politicization of Islam are constructed in diverse ways. For example, in the cases of both the Euro-Mediterranean Co-operation and the Muslim Brotherhood there are several common actors, but those cases are constructed each time according to a context's own inner logic. The impact of the same actors in the politicization process changes with context. Therefore, context has a crucial role in determining the content of actorness.

If we consider these actors' relationships to the politicization of Islam, the essential questions are: Who politicizes Islam or the existence of Islam? What actors in a particular context are relevant to the politicization of Islam? And whose action modifies the politicization process? All actors are not equally important, but no actor on its own can politicize things. Therefore, actors have different capabilities and possibilities to have an influence on or produce Islam. The actors' potential effects on politics and Islam are not equal, but they depend on different power structures.

This is why the Muslim Brotherhood, for example, cannot itself define how its activity in relation to Islam becomes politicized, i.e. it cannot determine its own relationship to Islam, even if it wanted to. The presence of other actors can cause undesired and unpredicted effects on the politicization process. This is clearly the case in the Euro-Mediterranean Co-operation.

The relevant collective forces are also heterogeneous, which means that the contacts between the members of the community depend on the factors conditioned by the context. In the case of the Muslim Brotherhood the community is basically built on personal contacts – or, in any event, those contacts are potentially possible. In that case the members of the community inhabit, in principle, the same geographical area (cf. Goonatilake 1991, 229–230). The members of the community formed on the Internet are not concretely in touch with each other (except in special cases) but only through technical mediums – digital media. The community exists virtually and on a global level but also through the action of individual members (cf. Goonatilake, 1991, 230). The Euro-Mediterranean Co-operation falls between these two extremes. It is regional and something that surpasses the borders of states, i.e. it is a *transnational* community. These definitions of community are tentative drafts and will be analyzed more thoroughly later in the book.

Cases may be classified as follows according to the aforementioned factors.

Case	Level of formality	Level of actorness	Nature of community
Euro-Mediterranean Co-operation	International politics; official	International	Transnational
Muslim Brotherhood	Sectoral politics; semi-official	"Face to face"	National group
Internet	Communicative; unofficial	Individual	Virtual

These cases are heterogeneous and therefore it is natural that Islam is politicized differently in each case. In relation to Islam, the intensity of processes of politicization varies, and the presence of Islam is dependent on how strongly Islam is articulated. Some cases may represent Islam more "strongly" than others because Islam is articulated in each example through different conditions.

More specific frame of study

Taking into account the previous discussion on the starting points for political research, identity and articulation, the focus throughout the rest of this book is:

- how these cases potentially represent political Islam
- what political articulations of Islam come up in these cases and how
- how identity is articulated, and the meaning of the self–other divide in this context
- what kind of community is enabled through the articulation of identity.

The case studies under scrutiny are quite dissimilar and therefore the material, the texts about these cases, is also quite diverse. In each case, the texts are selected according to their inner logic, and do not have much in common. Their form is different but the frame of study has been the basis of selection. In this sense they are somewhat alike because they give answers to the same kinds of questions.

PART II

1

The Euro-Mediterranean Co-operation: Participation and Legitimacy

Introduction

Throughout history, the Mediterranean area has shaped European reality and been an important part of it. In the same vein, the Mediterranean has been a route to eastern and southern coastal states. In that area different economic, political and cultural traditions and practices prevail, and regional interaction is rich and diverse, both in a positive and negative sense. Religions – Judaism, Christianity and Islam – have had their own role in this interaction and their importance have varied with times.

This chapter examines the co-operation between the European Union and non-Union Mediterranean countries and particularly *the Barcelona process*, which started at the beginning of 1995. The cornerstone of that process is the Euro-Mediterranean Partnership Declaration, an agreement that laid the framework for co-operation until the beginning of the new millennium. The starting point for the Barcelona process was the Euro-Mediterranean Conference, held in Barcelona in November 1995. The conference was attended by foreign ministers from 15 EU countries, and 12 eastern and southern Mediterranean countries: Morocco, Algeria, Tunisia, Egypt, Israel, Jordan, Lebanon, the Palestinian Authority, Syria, Turkey, Cyprus and Malta.[1] These countries will be called SEM countries (southern and eastern Mediterranean countries).

There were many reasons for organizing the Barcelona conference in 1995. The EU's policy on the Mediterranean already had a long tradition but results were not so satisfactory. The economic gulf between southern and eastern coasts was not reducing. According to the Commission: "[H]armonious economic and social development in the countries in question was still the long-term challenge" (Strengthening the Mediterranean Policy of the European Union, 1995, 18). However, some concrete results had already been received. For example, the access of industrial products into the EU had, in the Commission's view, created a positive impact in those countries that had executed economic reforms (Strengthening the Mediterranean Policy of the European Union, 1994, 7).

The aim of this chapter is to examine the meaning of Islam in the context of the Barcelona process. The Euro-Mediterranean Co-operation is an important research subject in the politicization of Islam, although the Barcelona process is not, characteristically, a religious context. Islam is, however, present in different levels of the process. The Euro-Mediterranean Co-operation is a good example of how Islam needs to be examined as a "relative" phenomenon; it should be evaluated without presuming that the case represents purely Islam.

Here I will focus on the Barcelona process as a whole – i.e. my view is on a multilateral level. This definition impacts on the selection and use of material. The preliminary material comprises the official texts and documents of the Barcelona process that are *joint* declarations of the EU and SEM countries. These offer a very original way of looking at the articulation of Islam because this form of articulation is not produced solely by "Islamic" actors.

Along with the official documents the material consists of those sources that are directly attached to the Barcelona process (for instance, speeches held in official meetings) or are in some other way part of the process (for instance, actions outside the official process and researchers' views of the process). This kind of material will present a picture of how the process is proceeding outside the state level. It will broaden the view and give background to the whole process.

Background to the Euro-Mediterranean Co-operation

Road to Barcelona

There is a long history of contact between Europe and the Mediterranean countries which dates back to before the Roman Empire. During the centuries the intensity of this contact has varied, but at no stage did it cease totally. The contemporary situation is largely based on the colonial period of the 19th and 20th centuries and its heritage.

The relationship of the EU and its predecessor, the European Community, to foreign countries has developed gradually as the internal integration of the EU has deepened. The co-operation of the EU and non-EU European countries began in the 1960s when the first bilateral agreements were made between individual countries. These agreements did not correspond to the spirit of the Treaty of Rome, and partially for that reason they were modified gradually so that by the end of the 1960s the contracting parties were the EU and separate Mediterranean countries (Ginsberg 1990, 119–120).

The bilateral phase continued until 1972 when the Global Mediterranean Policy (GMP) was introduced. This program covered the entire Mediterranean area. The GMP did not concentrate just on trade but also on financial co-operation, social questions, political dialogue and techno-scientific co-operation. In the late 1980s, the GMP came under some criticism, and in 1990 a new program, the New Mediterranean Policy, was introduced for the years 1992–1996 (Lorca and Nuñes 1993, 58). Some new elements were involved compared to the previous co-operation scheme which, despite opposite intentions, had concentrated on traditional forms and bilateral activity (On the Implementation of the Financial and Technical Cooperation, 1994, 16).

In the October 1994 communiqué the commission presented a view that the long-term strategy of the EU's co-operation was to create a Euro-Mediterranean Area. This referred to a politically stable and secure area where socioeconomic goals were taken into account (Strengthening the Mediterranean Policy of the European Union, 1994, 4). These outlines were taken further in Essen in December 1994 and in Cannes in June 1995. Those meetings were in preparation for the Barcelona Conference.

The central aim of the Barcelona Conference was to agree on the Barcelona Declaration, and the core idea was the Euro-Mediterranean Partnership. There are three main sections in the Barcelona Declaration: political, economic and sociocultural. This agreement combined, for the first time, all the areas in the framework of the Mediterranean Co-operation into one document. The objectives are very ambitious since many of those targets were, for the first time, under serious negotiation, and the negotiating parties were quite dissimilar.

Despite some disagreements in the preparation work and in agreeing on resolutions, the Barcelona process, and particularly its beginning, received a mostly positive response in both political and scientific circles. This was achieved by enlarging the process to cover as wide an area as possible. Especially taking account of the cultural and social affairs gave the Barcelona process a unique status in international co-operation. Usually, this kind of co-operation process rotates around trade and politics, and cultural and social matters are given only marginal attention or they are separated into their own block. In the Barcelona Declaration these sectors were at least formally given the same weight as other sectors of co-operation.

The Barcelona Declaration and the idea of partnership were not solely received with applause. Criticism was made concerning the impossibility of "real" partnership in an economic sense, because the economic development in northern and southern banks of the Mediterranean would, in any case, be asymmetric. There was a fear that institutionalized partnership meant in effect the hegemony of the north and dependency of the south (Makram-Ebeid, 1997, 3).

On the whole, the Mediterranean policy has, since the 1960s, been one of the most important foreign policy areas for the EU and its predecessor, the European Community. Especially in the 1990s, it was held as one of the cornerstones of the Common Foreign and Security Policy (CFSP), which was then being developed. It was an attempt to combine economic, trade and development policies along with non-military security measures under one policy. From the beginning, the economic side has been merged with security because the stability of the Mediterranean area is seen as an integral part of Europe's internal security. On the one hand, the Mediterranean is an interesting economic area but, on the other, it is understood as a potential threat to political stability and security.

Islam in post-Cold War Europe

The question of Islam received wide interest both before and after the Barcelona Conference. Islam was mentioned as one of the most important aspects for the whole process – especially concerning security and relations between Islam and the West. During the Cold War, the question of European security was mostly concerned with the actions of and relationship between the United States of America and the Soviet Union. It was assumed that any confrontation between these countries would take place on the European continent. Though these superpowers also had many other regional interests, the wish to control the old continent was the most typical feature in international politics during the Cold War (see Mortimer 1994, 105).

After the Cold War, European security thinking changed; the Mediterranean and Middle East areas became more interesting, and their position was re-evaluated. The EU had an enlargement in its agenda, after which its borders would be more discernible. Eberhard Rhein, a Commission official, analyzes the EU's strategic position like this:

> Early next century, the EU will essentially only have two major neighbours, the Russians in the East, the Arabs in the South. [...] The EU cannot afford socio-economic destabilization (or instability) of its immediate surroundings. This would inevitably spill over into the heart of Europe, not least through uncontrollable flows of illegal immigration (Rhein 1996, 80).

The strategic shift of the superpowers has clarified the EU's relationships with other areas. The importance of the former Soviet Union is no longer dependent on the USA; the relationship these days between the EU and Russia is more on a bilateral basis. Additionally, the Mediterranean area began to have more of an interest in its own right without its Cold War connections. This meant that the potential and problems of that region were seen more in relation to EU countries.

In this context, when world politics – and particularly the EU's foreign policy – was changing, there emerged the discussion of Islam as a "new threat to the West". It was the Americans who mainly generated the debate regarding Islam's position in international politics and as a possible threat; NATO was, for its own part, spreading this kind of thinking. In February 1995, when NATO presented its Mediterranean initiative, its (then) general secretary, Willy Claes, insisted that Muslim fundamentalism was the biggest threat since the collapse of Soviet communism (see e.g. Fenech 1997, 153).

This threat scenario received widespread attention and followed quite directly Samuel Huntington's idea of the clash of the civilizations (as already mentioned). In comparison, the European discussion on Islam has basically been different from the Huntingtonian view, which is relatively abstract. European's relationship with Muslim countries has, in many ways, been very concrete. Take, for instance, immigration and the immigrant Muslim communities in European cities: immigration, and especially illegal immigration, is seen as a problem with many faces, and Islam has its role to play in this. Expressions of Islamic politics of identity within the Muslim immigrant communities, in addition to high profile armed conflicts, have led to Islam becoming articulated into the European political agenda.

Controversy has been sparked by, for example, bomb attacks made by Islamic groups in Europe, the problems of Muslim communities with the state, and social unrest caused by the social problems of immigrants. Discussions both before and after the Barcelona Conference have, in many contexts, taken up the issues of "Muslim fundamentalism", "Muslim terrorism" and other similar phenomena. Thus, the general "Muslim threat" rhetoric received its concrete form in "fundamentalism" which, depending on the particular case, was directly connected to Islam, shown to be a byproduct of Islam or separated totally from "genuine" Islam.

Simultaneously, other themes were involved with Europe's own Islam debate such as: the first Gulf War (1991), the case of Salman Rushdie (which is more fully explained on page 134) and internal problems in several countries that involved Muslim activity. These cases have created an international Islam discourse that follows the logic of Huntington's scheme on the clash of civilizations – though the basis for the argument is different from the American context. Whether or not Islam is a real political threat, for several years it has nevertheless been an important factor in the internal Western political discourse as well as in the discourse between the West and Muslim countries. This was something borne in mind during the introduction and implementation of the Barcelona process.

Islam as a manifestation of culture
The cultural basis of the Barcelona Declaration
The discussion that preceded the Barcelona Conference led to an understanding that Islam would be seen in a negative light during the Barcelona process. However, the Barcelona process did somewhat widen the possibilities of articulation into other areas. One central area is culture. In the Barcelona Declaration itself there is no mention of religions, but they are implicitly included in the declaration and are explicitly present in other levels of the process.

Thus, even if Islam and other religions are not mentioned in the Barcelona Declaration, it does not mean that religions and culture are not present in the process. Quite the opposite: certain cultural, and therefore religious, expressions are repeated many times both in the Barcelona Declaration and in many other connected texts and agendas.

The cultural starting point in the Barcelona Declaration is that cultural characteristics at the state level and between states should be strengthened and encouraged in the co-operation:

> [The participants of the conference] resolved to establish to that end a multilateral and lasting framework of relations based on a spirit of partnership, with due regard for the characteristics, values and distinguishing features peculiar to each of the participants;
>
> [participants undertake to] develop the rule of law and democracy in their political systems, while recognizing in this framework the right of each of them to choose and freely develop its own political, socio-cultural, economic and judicial system;
>
> [participants] reaffirm that dialogue and respect between cultures and religions are a necessary pre-condition for bringing the peoples closer. In this connection they stress the importance of the role the mass media can play in the reciprocal recognition and understanding of cultures as a source of mutual enrichment;
>
> [participants] stress the essential nature of the development of human resources, both as regards the education and training of young people in particular and in the area of culture. They express their intent to promote cultural exchanges and knowledge of other languages, respecting the cultural identity of each partner, and to implement a lasting policy of educational and cultural programmes; in this context, the partners undertake to adopt measures to facilitate human exchanges, in particular by improving administrative procedures (Euro-Mediterranean Conference, 1995).

There is a purpose in the Declaration to build a coherent unity where participants have different demands and where structures of the state are dissimilar. From the basis of this diversity, there is an attempt to build *understanding and dialogue between cultures*. The general tone of the Declaration is moderate and also quite unspecific. Cultural factors are not explicitly stated, but one can interpret that the role of religions is seen as important for cultural identity. Various practical programs support different cultural objectives. The general formulation of the Declaration gets a more concrete wording in the working program of the Barcelona Declaration:

> Because it is important to develop mutual understanding by promoting cultural exchange and language skills, officials and experts will meet to propose concrete actions on following fields: cultural and art heritage, cultural and art performances, joint productions (theater

and film), translations and other means of cultural dissemination, and education.[2]

In addition to the Barcelona Declaration and its working program, the cultural aspect has been under serious consideration in many academic and non-political connections. It should be understood, though, that the views expressed by these actors outside the official process would not "directly" influence the articulation of Islam as defined by SEM countries and the EU. It is relevant, however, to take into account these outside actors because they show that the contents of the Barcelona Declaration are not random in relation to the views of other actors interested in this area. The unofficial part of the Barcelona process, though, was strengthening and directing the results of the official process.

The most important cultural forum outside the official program of the Barcelona process has been the Forum Civil Euro-Med, which held its own meeting alongside the Barcelona 1995 conference and the Malta 1997 conference. The forum has also been quite active outside of these meetings. It is an NGO-based activity and on the whole there have been more heterogeneous and critical opinions and views than those offered by the official partnership program, although the basic starting points of the forum are largely the same as in the Barcelona Declaration:

> One of the objectives of the debate consisted of recommending *inter-religious dialogue*, a key element that should be very much taken into account. It is a case of promoting closer cultural links between Mediterranean societies through the religious traditions of Islam, Christianity and Judaism (forum civil euromed 1996, 180).

The quantitative growth of the discourses attached to culture is significant if it is compared to the contents and structure of the previous Mediterranean Co-operation. One can even talk about conscious over-emphasizing of culture. These practical applications of the declaration and the discourse it produced comply generally with the Declaration, and dissident and critical voices have been relatively few.

Especially for the SEM countries, the cultural co-operation signified in principle more equal or at least much extensive co-operation, because areas other than economy and politics were involved. The implicated countries are not basically thought of only as producers of raw materials, something that would be taken advantage of. The co-operation can be interpreted as an attempt to eliminate colonial attitudes towards the non-EU Mediterranean countries. The EU wants to underline that the cultural background, the sources of identity and characteristic features of SEM countries, will be taken into account in the Barcelona context, and emphasis is on "genuine" partnership which would not be based on former development co-operation mentality (see Euro-Mediterranean Partnership, European Commission 1997, 8).

The Barcelona Declaration is quite straightforward in the articulation of Islam. Though there is no mention of Islam or other religions in the cultural part of the Declaration, it is obvious that Islam is referred to, as are other religions of the Mediterranean area. Islam is naturally articulated with culture but it is not self-evident, as one can see from the "Islam is a threat" speeches. This kind of cultural articulation consciously depoliticizes Islam; it does not give room for political articulation of religion.

Islam and other religions are, however, more than "mere" religions that define personal relationships to religious worship or life hereafter. Religion is seen through collective participation, and therefore it defines something more than an individual's life. The articulation of religion through collective experience and participation means that religion as a phenomenon is significant also in an international co-operation context such as the Barcelona process.

Static and dynamic interpretations of culture
Cultures and religions are articulated in the Barcelona process relatively clearly at different levels – both in the official multilateral part and in unofficial circles. In the whole process, culture and religion have a significant role as those sectors of social life that have importance not only on a local level but also in an international context. They are not self-evidently involved in the process, whose primary objectives are in economic and security sectors. In the Mediterranean Co-operation cultures and religions have not been articulated distinctly during the history of the co-operation. Therefore it is interesting and significant, at a general level, that the cultural aspect is taken into account in the co-operation. How are cultures and religions then seen in the Barcelona process? My interpretation is that it is seen in two opposite ways: statically and dynamically.

The static way of interpreting cultures suggests that cultures are objects to which certain actions are directed. In relation to cultural matters, the general tone of the Barcelona Declaration emphasizes a historical perspective. The treatment of culture is quite conservative and distant: culture must be "preserved", "improved", or "respected".

The Declaration and accompanying programs for action give an impression that culture is something that developed a long time ago, and which nowadays must be "conserved" and "brought into a museum". One good example of this is the declaration of the Euro-Mediterranean cultural heritage given by the cultural ministers of the EU and the partnership countries in the ministerial conference in Bologna in 1996:

> [...] the 27 culture ministers reaffirmed their recognition of respective cultural traditions and called for a strengthening of the cultural dialogue. The aim of the meeting was to reinforce dialogue on joint cultural matters, as well as to launch concrete projects of a regional nature which will focus on preserving and exploiting cultural heritage.
>
> In line with the Bologna declaration, these concrete projects should take effect in one of the following areas:
> - knowledge of the heritage through the dissemination of the information, awareness raising among the public and decision-makers, and cataloguing of heritage, know-how and techniques; [...]
> - the exploitation of heritage through cataloguing and networking of historical sites which are used as places of beauty, as well as the promotion of tourism (Euro-Mediterranean Partnership, information note No. 8).

These kinds of statements show that the existence of a non-European culture in the Barcelona process is acceptable. The existence of European culture is not separately emphasized: it is inherently present. The non-European culture can be objectivized to a suitable form, and particularly one acceptable and understandable for Europeans. This setting could be compared to Henrietta Riegel's interpretation of museums: the visitor is moving but the objects are "lifeless" (Riegel 1996, 86).

For the EU, the culture and cultural objects of the southern and eastern Mediterranean are usually objects that are eternal and unchanging. The EU is what is dynamic and moving, and it upholds this structure. Objectivization is, in practice, directed to monuments and other historical and material "remnants". But the idea of objectivization is not unfamiliar in connection with religions, which are considered to be part of cultural heritage. Religions are also seen as static constructions, which define the identity of their object field. They represent something characteristic and essential, and preserving them is connected to the definitions of existence.

The static approach objectivizes cultures and religions, but especially in relation to religions there is a more dynamic approach available where they are seen more as functional entities. Culture has its role in increasing the understanding between different countries and areas. In the Mediterranean, the major religions – Christianity, Islam and Judaism – have their particular role in this. Religions may act as a mediator in the dialogue between civilizations, and the Barcelona process can be part of this by creating necessary institutional structures (Makram-Ebeid 1997, 5–7). Cultures are given a certain function: when we understand other cultures we understand each other and there will not be so many problems. In this process, religions have a vital role:

> Greater understanding among the major religions present in the Euro-Mediterranean region will facilitate greater mutual tolerance and co-operation. Support will be given to periodic meetings of representatives of religions and religious institutions as well as theologians, academics and others concerned, with the aim of breaking down prejudice, ignorance and fanaticism and fostering co-operation at grass-roots level. The conferences held in Stockholm (15–17 June 1995) and Toledo (4–7 November 1995) may serve as examples in this context (Euro-Mediterranean Conference, 1995).

In this quote, one can see the status between the north and the south: there are prejudices and ignorance but they should be kept in control and co-operation should be increased. The interesting point is that the religions particularly are thought to have some role in solving this problem. Therefore, one can come to the conclusion that the problems themselves are thought to be connected to religious factors: the problems are perceived essentially to be religious even if, for instance, "fanaticism" has more to do with sociopolitical structures than religious–theological factors.

The articulation of religions produced by the EU and SEM countries is repeated in other elements that are more connected to the process. For instance, the attitude of the Forum Civil Euro-Med towards the role of religion is much the same as in the official program. At the Malta meeting, the Forum published a revealing background paper in which official statements on the importance of the dialogue between cultures and the role of religions is repeated:

> To emphasise the need to foster better mutual understanding through cultural exchange and religious tolerance. To reaffirm the message of the Barcelona Conference that dialogue between cultures and religions is a fundamental requirement for drawing peoples together, as well as for partnership and co-operation. [...] To overcome prejudices and thus attain deeper mutual knowledge. To promote cultural exchanges and knowledge of other cultures, respecting the cultural identity of each partner (Background note: "Intercultural Dialogue: A Basis for Co-operation", 1997).

Religions are the arena in which mutual understanding takes place and the representatives of religions are actors that are, in practice, building the discourse of understanding. It is interesting to see that the process of building the understanding is connected to cultures and religions, not for instance to political or economic dialogue. In my view, the reason for this is that cultures and religions form a neutral enough forum where it is not necessary to take a position on the most critical issues, such as the Middle East peace process. Cultures and religions are, though, sufficiently relevant elements in the Mediterranean context.

Even if culture is given a purpose outside of the cultural sector as a potential motor for mutual understanding, it is still clearly separated from other aspects of co-operation – for instance, from the political sector. Culture has, to some degree, been seen in the European context in a Huntingtonian way (the articulation of possible cultural conflict through culture) but still the conflictual articulation of culture is avoided in the Barcelona process. Culture is seen as stable at a national level – something that supports existing social structures, not so much as a renewing force. However, in an international context, culture has been given – as already mentioned – a mission to increase mutual understanding.

It should still be understood that for the SEM countries cultural matters are not neutral or politically non-articulated; they could be linked to national reform pressures in the level of civil society, for example. George Joffé suggests that a freer exchange of information is "unpleasant" for some governments because information is not easy to control. This means, according to Joffé, that these governments are suspicious of the culture and social paragraphs because these encourage direct contacts between independent groups and NGOs, and threatens the governmental control (Joffé 1997, 27).

Therefore, it is suitable for SEM countries to interpret the cultural paragraphs of the Barcelona Declaration in a narrow sense. Culture would thus be seen as a stable entity ready to be taken to the museum, rather than as a possible *national* catalyst for social change. Culture and Islam are not considered as a forum of politics. Islam will not become a visible part of politics, even if it is given a considerable weight. The importance of Islam can be seen in various programs that are linked to the Barcelona process where Islam is explicitly present. In the examples mentioned earlier, one can see the same theme of isolating Islam, as in the Barcelona Declaration itself. In the context of the Barcelona process, Islam is seldom mentioned as a political phenomenon, even if the idea is in the background.

Excursus: Islam, culture and the construction of European identity

The Barcelona process is not only revealing for the SEM countries. It is also an indication of how European identity is built in this kind of international context. Foreign cultures and religions have an intriguing role in constructing identity. These kinds of processes strengthen the identities of both partners: mutual interaction helps to define the borderline between self and other. Thus, Islam is also relevant in defining European identity, not just for the identities of Muslim countries. Put another way: the constitution of European identity is significant in shaping perceptions of the identities of the SEM countries.

Before I examine in more detail the political Islamic identity of SEM countries, I will undertake a short excursus concerning the birth of European identity from the point of view of the Barcelona process and the EU. The EU has many intentional ways of building identity, which are meant to express the common features of European identity. These include respecting democracy, humanism and the principle of freedom. The EU has also tried to present and regularly use certain symbols that, for their own part, aim to build awareness of being European. Examples include the Union's star flag, the hymn ("Ode to Joy") and Europe Day (9 May).

Non-intentional ways of building European identity are included in the structures of the Union's work and its different forms. Here, the EU's attempt to build common foreign and security policy is especially important because through it the Union defines its relationships to outside countries and areas. The question of identity is connected to the whole structure of the EU's foreign relations. When the EU wants to construct common foreign and security policy, it is to comment on the questions: 'What are we?' 'What do we want?' 'What are we not?' and 'What do we not want?' The limits of its own existence are then defined in relation to actors outside itself, i.e. European identity will partly be defined through negation. As Neumann and Welsch conclude:

> The very idea of Europe was from the beginning defined to a certain extent in terms of what it was not. In other words, the other, i.e., the non-European barbarian or savage, played a decisive role in evolution of the European identity (Neumann and Welsch 1991, 329).

In my view, the idea of European identity manifests itself most distinctly in cultural factors. In practical terms, this means that when the EU is defining its common interests and the limits of European identity it is concerned ultimately with cultural factors, rather than economics or politics. The most important concrete objectives of the EU are naturally connected to economy, politics and security, but the symbolic level of European identity is mostly defined by culture.

The cultural part of the Barcelona process is one way of producing European identity in relation to the "otherness". In it are defined those things that do no belong to Europeanism. When referring to SEM countries, the Barcelona Declaration uses words like "special characteristics" or "special nature". This indicates that the EU's partner is different from "us", and we must take account of this difference. If somebody was similar to us, then we would not have to respect "special characteristics" or "nature" because they would be seen like us, and common characteristics would be underlined. The emphasis, though, is on the fact that the other has characteristics that are not like ours.

Here, SEM countries could be compared to Middle and Eastern European countries. For instance, Poland's possible EU membership is seen as part of a historical process in which the Middle and Eastern European countries rid themselves of the continental division that has lasted more than 40 years, so Poland can unite with the EU to bring "peace, stability and prosperity" to this area (see Agenda 2000). Incorporating Poland and other countries into the EU means in a certain way fulfilling the historically significant task in which countries that have been separated for some time are being reconnected to the European family.

Even if the EU says it will respect the views and circumstances of SEM countries, one can consider whether the EU's attitude towards the outside world is fundamentally different from, for instance, the European political actors' attitude in the era of colonialism. SEM countries are hardly considered acceptable to join the EU, even if they wanted to. These countries are not thought of as part of European existence, but they are suitable as trading partners. In addition to this, maintaining confidential and friendly relations is important for the EU for the sake of regional security and peace. SEM countries will, of course, benefit from trade and security. That said, the co-operation is primarily undertaken according to the EU's terms and interests.

Understanding the identity of SEM countries in the context of the Barcelona process is closely connected to the action of the EU. The EU is not a neutral actor whose objectives would totally lack, for example, aspects linked to identity. In the Barcelona process European identity stays in the background, and otherness is not built consciously in a conflictual way. This means that, for instance, Islam and other cultural matters are not intentionally seen in a negative light.

In spite of this, the foreign policy model of the EU – especially the CFSP, of which the Euro-Mediterranean Co-operation is one example – includes in a structural sense the project of building a European unity. In order to come true, the CFSP needs jointly approved targets, through which are made assumptions of individual interests and the basis for them. Because the issue is taking care of foreign relations, there are simultaneously made assumptions and evaluations of a political target or targets, which in this case refers to SEM countries and their identities. Therefore, the productive role of power in constituting identity is very obvious: the EU defines for its own part the formation of the identity of SEM countries in its foreign policy.

These assumptions and evaluations made by Europe are essentially important in thinking through the constitution of Islamic identity in the Barcelona process. As mentioned earlier, the identity is constructed in an interaction in which otherness is a necessary and inevitable part. Islam and other cultural features of SEM countries are both a relevant and historically understandable way to outline the construction of European identity. The Barcelona process is a special context, because it combines the potential of developing both European and Islamic identities.

Islam as a source of national identity

The cultural part of the Barcelona Declaration shows how cultures and religions are seen in the Euro-Mediterranean context. Islam is a part of national culture, and thus religion has its own role in understanding and constructing the lives and identity of Muslim countries. The self-understanding of Muslim countries is therefore also produced in this cultural discourse. Islam is situated in a certain category and will be given "tasks" that are approved by SEM countries and the EU.

In the Barcelona process, Islam and the role of religions is considered to be important in constructing identity, too. I would nonetheless see this identity to be cultural and ethnic rather than political. Islam is articulated in this process, but these articulations are non-conflictual. The self-understanding of SEM countries is constructed this way, but it is not the primary objective in politicization in relation to the EU, and it is not a method to form differences with the "otherness".

According to Pierre Hassner, the Western concept of nationality has traditionally constitutional expressions that are based on nation, territory, nationality and political principles (Hassner 1993, 60). In my view, the Barcelona process reflects that part of the national identity of SEM countries that is based on ethnicity. Hassner calls this the "Eastern" concept. The idea of nationality based on an ethnic background is associated with common culture that is defined by race, language, tradition and/or religion.

SEM countries may be quite different in relation to Islam, and its importance to people's lives can vary tremendously. Despite this, these countries have a somewhat similar understanding of religion, and can therefore communicate with the help of symbolic meanings, metaphors and narratives that are associated with religion; people who belong to this cultural context understand discussion on religion (see Sanders 1997, 184–185). The cultural meanings of religion are not by themselves connected to an individual's religious beliefs, but, for instance, to how religion represents the essence of state and nation.

In the Barcelona process, Islam is given the sense of building a national existence. For SEM countries, Islam means in this process the same as the concepts of democracy, liberty and liberalism for European states as the interpreter of the national essence. Here we can talk, at least in a limited sense, about civil religion, where the relation between state and religion or nation and religion is very close. In the Barcelona process, Islam is regarded as a phenomenon that portrays and explains the national existence of SEM countries. The legitimacy of a nation is partly based on religious grounds.

In the context of the Barcelona process Islam gets an approved form. The important point is that the approval comes – because of the multilateral nature of co-operation – also through actions and objectives of the EU. The EU's habit of emphasizing the meaning of Islam and culture gives a legitimate opportunity to create a national identity of the Muslim state because that way Islam is channeled to non-political elements of social life. According to this interpretation, the Islam in question differs from the Islam that is connected to terrorism and other potentially threatening forms of Islam.

The actions of Muslim states in the Euro-Mediterranean Co-operation take places mainly in relation to EU countries, not to other Muslim states. This indicates that the logic of actions comes through the whole of multilateral co-operation, although the EU determines it. The policy of the Muslim states is therefore rather more reactive than productive: it largely follows the EU's agenda and Muslim countries have little to say in this.

One must remember, though, that Muslim countries agree to co-operation in order to gain trade and security benefits. Thus, it could be argued that both SEM countries and the EU depoliticized Islam in the Barcelona process, and the form of co-operation defines the construction of Islamic identity. The Euro-Mediterranean Co-operation is not, then, as likely a context for politicizing Islamic identity than those contexts that are between the Muslim countries.

In the Barcelona context, facing otherness is not a purely negative process. There is a dialogic interaction and non-Europeans are given a chance for their voice to be heard. But negotiations with the other may rise from the desire to take hold of otherness in some way. Then, dialogue can be a means of materializing the other (see Väyrynen 1997, 71). Although SEM countries are, in principle, equal partners with the EU in the Euro-Mediterranean Co-operation, they do not construct their identity independently and the power relation with the EU crucially determines the self-understanding of SEM countries.

It should be noticed that there are elements in the Mediterranean Co-operation that support the construction of Islamic political identity. The actions of the EU are important in this sense. Although the EU considers that cultures basically have a positive role in the Barcelona process, the logic of constructing the European identity is largely based on otherness. In Europe's eyes, a non-European culture is an alien culture, and dissimilarities are emphasized but possible similarities are not registered. Religion is, in this context, one of the most important factors in creating differences.

EU, Islam and terrorism

Terrorism and regional instability

The cultural articulation of Islam seems to indicate that Islam is a factor that unites Muslim countries internally; that it would give some common ground for actions and existence. In the process of "culturalizing" Islam, it is therefore given the task of serving the national unity. The guarantors of this unity are the governments and political elites involved in the process. This articulated positive role of Islam – the "accepted" Islam – is, however, strictly limited: at a national level, Islam has no other legitimate chances to exist in the Barcelona process. However, Islam has another particular referent: besides culture, Islam is also connected to terrorism and its political articulation.

The word "terrorism" is used very carefully in the Barcelona process. The use of this term has clearly been avoided in official contexts so that it could not be connected to any particular country or to any particular form of terrorism. From Islam's point of view, the Barcelona Declaration and affiliated actions and programs become interesting at this point. Although Islam is not directly mentioned, it is clear that there are references in the Declaration to religious and especially Islamic political movements.[3] This assumption is based on, among other things, the discussions both before and after the meeting in which Islam was directly connected to the actions of different extremist movements in SEM countries and inside the EU.

There has been an attempt to bring terrorism to the agenda of the Barcelona process in order to gain government involvement to suppress terrorism and thus use this process in fighting terrorism. For example, the Barcelona Declaration states:

[The participants undertake to] strengthen their co-operation in preventing and combating terrorism, in particular by ratifying and applying the international instruments they have signed, by acceding to such instruments and by taking any other appropriate measure; [...]

[the participants] agree to strengthen co-operation by means of various measures to prevent terrorism and fight it together more effectively (Euro-Mediterranean Conference, 1995).

The Declaration itself is quite laconic with regard to terrorism; it is given serious consideration but the concept of terrorism is not defined, and there are no suggestions as to how to fight it. However, the working program of the Declaration placed things at a firmer level by giving recommendations and instructions for further actions:

Fighting terrorism will have to be a priority for all the parties. To that end, officials will meet periodically with the aim of strengthening co-operation among police, judicial and other authorities. In this context, consideration will be given, in particular, to stepping up exchanges of information and improving extradition procedures.

Officials will meet periodically to discuss practical measures which can be taken to improve co-operation among police, judicial, customs, administrative and other authorities in order to combat, in particular, drug trafficking and organized crime, including smuggling.

All these meetings will be organized with due regard for the need for a differentiated approach that takes into account the diversity of the situation in each country (Euro-Mediterranean Conference, 1995).

The proposed actions aim to control terrorism, integrating this target into mutual co-operation. Fighting terrorism is mainly a police matter. The task is to develop structures for controlling the problem.

Among SEM countries, terrorism is most often connected to Israel and the Palestinian Authority, and also to Lebanon, Egypt, Algeria and Turkey. From the SEM countries' point of view, it is a question of the threat inside their own borders that is aimed towards the governments. There is a secondary fear that the terrorism in one country would spread to neighboring countries. The EU, however, fears the threat that is aimed towards Europe itself. The threat to security is potentially present inside the borders of Europe in the form of Muslim immigrants, for example. Second, the regional instability caused by terrorism is suspected to endanger the possibility of exploiting natural resources, which would have indirect consequences for Europe, too. Therefore, terrorism has a cumulative effect on the area north of the Mediterranean (see e.g. King and Donati 1999, 150, Joffé 1994, 30–31 and Tovias 1996, 9). The EU is thus not concerned particularly or solely with those countries in which this kind of terrorism occurs. In all, the question of terrorism is connected to regional security, to which Islamic movements are considered a threat.

Even though using the word "terrorism" caused disagreements in the Barcelona meeting, it was accepted into the final draft of the Barcelona Declaration. It could be interpreted that the SEM countries had, after all, the same attitude towards terrorism as the EU. The essential thing here is that different sides had a *common interest* in opposing something they defined as terrorism.[4] This would not be so important in the whole process unless it did not also involve national connotations that receive meanings through the international context in question.

The Barcelona process, economy and Islam

The Barcelona process contributes, for its part, to fighting and preventing terrorism. It is also possible to take another view on terrorism: the question is how the Barcelona process can, in the longer term, *advance the rise of terrorism* connected to Islam. It is not just a question of a present – and solvable – problem, it is also a phenomenon that can evolve because of the Barcelona process and the actions involved in it.

There have been fears that the Barcelona process cannot deliver what it promises, but will instead create new problems. The process has been criticized for its inability to solve the social, economic and regional problems of some countries (see e.g. Joffé, 1997). Bichara Khader criticizes the EU's actions in the Barcelona process because he thinks they clearly have negative effects on the economies of SEM countries and on their socioeconomic situation. Khader argues that in spite of good intentions the Barcelona process cannot fulfill plans for greater prosperity and stability (interview with Khader, 16 December 1997).

According to Khader, the negative economic consequences of the Barcelona process will create socioeconomic problems in SEM countries, and those problems may be expressed in the form of Islamism. In Khader's view, the origins of political movements are connected to these kinds of problems, and therefore the Barcelona process can work against its own objectives (interview with Khader, 16 December 1997; c.f. Kienle, 1998).

Free trade and the Barcelona process can, in the short term, have positive effects, but if those effects are even smaller than is thought, then the continuation of the process is hampered.

The "official" view of the Barcelona process is, however, that as a whole it will provide the possibility of preventing terrorism. For instance, the statement by the Commission's official, Eberhard Rhein, demonstrates the EU's firm belief that the Barcelona process will bring stability, and that Islamists, among others, are a threat to that stability:

> There will be efforts to foil the whole process by religious or political fanatics who refuse to accept the harsh realities of the planet in the twenty-first century, and by those groups who are afraid of losing their traditional privileges. But in the end, reality will prevail, and it will be accepted that there is no better alternative than that of Euro-Mediterranean Partnership striving to work for a lasting zone of peace and stability in this tiny part of the planet, which has been the source both of endless conflict and of unique cultural achievement (Rhein 1996, 86).

According to Jon Marks, the creation of the free trade area in the Mediterranean is one example of how, in the 1990s, there was a tendency to create broad transnational trade and investment complexes through which closer political and sociocultural relations were to be built (Marks 1996, 2). With economic reforms and programs, the economies of SEM countries will be developed, and in that way social conditions also improved. In the longer term, this would calm the political situation, and thus the growth of Islamism (or even its very existence) could be eliminated.

Monopolization of Islam, national legitimacy and democracy

Whether the Barcelona process solves the problems of terrorism or produces them, the countries involved have had a keen interest in the matter. Religiously colored political activity and its potentially violent forms are seen as a common enemy both for the EU and the governments of SEM countries. This is why there is a common will to resolve the matter in some way or at least bring it to the political agenda so that possible actions could somehow be justified or legitimated. The countries in this process have, therefore, similar objectives but it should be understood that their purposes are different. This stems from the fact that the consequences of this policy and the meanings attached to it can in some sense be unpredictable.

When we talk about terrorism, it is crucial to understand the definition and contents of that concept: to recognize, in other words, when an action is judged to be terrorism rather than "normal" political activity. Alex Schmid defines terrorism as:

> [A]n anxiety-inspiring method of repeated violent action, employed by (semi) clandestine individual groups or state actors, for idiosyncratic, criminal or political reasons, whereby – in contrast to assassination – the direct targets of violence are not the main targets (Schmid, quoted in Badey 1998, 91).

Typical of terrorism is the threatening and random nature of violence: in principle it can hit anyone. This basic idea provides a good picture of the nature of terrorism, but there is one problem: how to define terrorists. If groups or actors are *presumed* to be terrorists, then they are classified as terrorists, and fighting terrorism is directed at *potential* terrorists.

At this point, the definition of Muslim terrorism and its existence in the Barcelona process becomes interesting. It is easy to attach the stamp of Muslim terrorism to various political actors in Muslim countries because widespread discourse connected to Muslim terrorism can be utilized both inside SEM countries and in Europe. Political violence – articulated in an Islamic way, for instance – is not unknown in any of the SEM countries but a broad definition of terrorism could affect those political actors, too, which should not be included (c.f. Fuller and Lesser 1995, 118). If, for instance, the actions of Islamic movements are categorically defined as terrorism, then the existing space for political activity will be reduced.

Legitimacy and monopolizing Islam
Islam is a channel to legitimacy both for the states and to the groups challenging them. Historically, the justified existence of Muslim states in the Mediterranean, the national legitimacy, is strongly based on Islam (see Hermassi 1993, 102). However, the postcolonial era meant that the problem of legitimacy surfaced strongly, and in this context there emerged an ideological basis for the state other than Islam – for example, Arabism, Arab nationalism and Marxism.

Several internal problems of relating to SEM countries are still attached to legitimacy, and particularly to the lack of it. Internal difficulties and conflicts, such as the powerlessness of opposition and weak attendance at elections, are typical for governments or states that have problems with their legitimacy. The elites in power are more or less closed entities, and they cannot be regarded as ready for change. The political activity of Islamists is one reaction to the crisis of legitimacy: they represent the opposition forces that try to challenge the government's illegitimate position from their point of view (see e.g. Aliboni 1996, 1). For these movements the governments are therefore not reliable or legitimate political actors, and movements are forms of opposition or resistance.

The dilemma lies in the legitimacy of those governments, which is perceived differently in various fora. In the context of the Barcelona process these governments represent the sole legitimate actors for the EU, especially in relation to Islam. Surpassing and mixing the different levels of action means that the EU is also influencing – unintentionally, it seems – the domestic policy of Muslim countries because the effects of the Barcelona process naturally spread to a national level.

What does this means to the existence of Islam? One way in which governments have taken power and legitimacy away from Islamic groups has been to limit the appearance of "public" Islam to an official level. This has meant taking control of mosques and other religious institutions – in other words, they have been "nationalized". Here we can talk of monopolizing Islam, which means that governmental actors are taking over the symbols and institutions connected to Islam.[5] This monopolization of Islam has occurred in several countries, though there are national characteristics as well.

In the 1990s, Tunisia was regarded as a moderate and peaceful country in relation to Islam and to different forms of political Islam. However, that situation was the result of many measures that restricted Islam. The mosques and *imams* were controlled, and national television was used to teach Islam and convey the calls to prayer (Grimaud 1996, 100–101). The situation in Egypt was, in general, similar.

The situation in Morocco, with regard to Islam and Islamism, is somewhat different from Tunisia or Egypt, the reason being the position of the king. The king is thought to be the descendant of the Prophet Mohammed, which gives him a greatly respected authority in Morocco (Willis 1996, 18). The control of Islam in Morocco is thus based on historical tradition, rather than on recent political actions. The effects, however, may be similar, and thus Islamic politics can be pursued only by those political actors that are clearly attached to the government or the monarch.

The attitude of the Turkish government to Islam was quite intriguing in the 1990s. The Islamic Party was in power for a short period but since then Turkey has taken a tough stance on Islam and politics, which the government tries to keep separate. Behind this position lies Turkey's desire to present itself as a Western and secular state in order to retain credibility as a candidate for EU membership. The state has tried to define the relation between politics and religion in such a manner that excludes Islamic political actors. However, the ruling elite have not tried to take advantage of the religious symbolism or arguments.

The common factor in these cases is that the state-level actors do not want to give Islamists the opportunity to use Islam to their own advantage. In some situations, reacting against Islamism means, in fact, that the state "returns" (at least to some degree) to Islam in order to gain legitimacy. In other cases, the state has taken a conscious and clear secular direction, as in Turkey. Common for these countries, in any case, is that states try to get hold of Islam in some way or another.

The monopolization of Islam by the state is one way of controlling the political activity that is linked to Islam or articulated through Islam. The question here is not just about controlling Islam but also about controlling political space and possibilities. Citing Fahmi Huweidy, one can talk about monopolizing politics in a situation where the state tries to overtake religious symbols and practices (interview with Huweidy, 3 March 1997). Then the state is using religion for political purposes. In that case we can talk – at least in a narrow sense – of using religion as a political tool, and the state seeing itself as the only official mouthpiece of religion.

Democracy and Islam

Monopolizing politics and narrowing the space of politics has a direct influence on the domestic policies of SEM countries. These questions also influence other themes in the Barcelona process, particularly the question of democracy. With regards the Barcelona process, (Islamic) terrorism cannot be seen as a separate phenomenon or problem that will be solved in some way, because terrorism as a phenomenon is connected to the national policies of SEM countries (cf. Calleya 1998, 57). This is why comparing the prevention of terrorism and the demand for democracy in the Barcelona Declaration sheds an interesting light on the subject: democracy and terrorism are not dealt with in the same context but as completely separate phenomena.

For instance, the actions of Islamists shows how their channels for participation in the political processes are limited because those groups are seen to have close connections to terrorists or they are just considered to be a threat to democracy. Thus, the situation is seen as a very black-and-white affair in the Barcelona process. One possibility is to support the governments that are seen as the guarantors of democracy, and by doing so suffocate the actions of Islamic groups. In this case, striving to maintain the status quo both in the region and inside the states is important (cf. Bouchat 1996, 345). Broadening the avenues of participation towards Islamic groups is interpreted as slipping into an undemocratic situation. According to this kind of thinking, Islamists represent automatically and by definition the undemocratic forces.

There is an inevitable double standard in defining the relationship between democracy and Islam in the Barcelona process. Islamism is repressed by means that are questionable for the democracy. It is allowed, however, because Islamists are seen as representing even more undemocratic forces. The fact that opening up democratic process to Islamists does not mean they will automatically step into power is ignored, because voters are not necessarily backing them. Nevertheless, if people vote Islamists into power, it will follow the principles of representative democracy.

The EU's partly one-sided attitude to Islam and to different Islamic actors is connected to the inner logic of the Barcelona process: the co-operation does not give in itself the possibility of a more nuanced approach to Islam. The problem also is the EU's limited ability to judge and examine Islam as a political issue. The EU has, for some time, concentrated its own policy into other more acute topics and has been forced to evaluate its own existence at the expense of its foreign policy. Therefore, the EU does not necessarily have enough experience and political will to discuss Islamic political activity. In addition to this, each EU country is so different that it is not easy to form a common policy towards Islam. Different countries have historically diverse relationships with Muslim countries and, for instance, the importance and role of Muslim immigrants varies from one country to another.

The difficulty the EU finds in handling political Islam means, in fact, that it cannot necessarily, and nor does it want to, predict what kind of effects the Barcelona process can have on the different forms of political Islam. Though activities regarded as Muslim terrorism would be a common enemy to the EU and SEM countries, suffocating terrorism means different things to these two entities. For the EU, it would mean primarily eliminating a factor that threatens the EU's own security. For SEM countries, it would also mean suppressing the (potential) political opposition.

Monopolizing Islam, legitimacy and democracy have a close yet contradictory connection. The ability of the states to define the possibilities for articulating Islam in the Barcelona process means also defining the just and approved Islamic actors. This, on the other hand, means articulating the legitimacy relations partly through Islam. In relation to the EU, the state level of SEM countries represents a legitimate force that can define Islam in a just manner. However, the national-level Islamic actors question by their own action the legitimacy of the states.

Regarding the activities of Islamic movements as terrorism gives way to creating a confined political space, at which point the question of the principles of a democratic system arises: Is defining Islamic movements as terrorist and banning them in accordance with democracy or not? What is more important in the Barcelona process: to have a common definition of democracy *or* of terrorism?

Muslim identity between national and international

The articulation of Islam and terrorism in the Barcelona process is important in thinking about the identities of the actors involved in it. The negative identifications of terrorism are naturally attached to Islamic actors who are regarded as terrorists or promoters of terrorism. They are mainly Islamic movements and their members in SEM countries and potentially in the EU countries. In the Barcelona process, the identity of "Islamic terrorists" is seen as constructed by violent articulations, and should therefore be dealt with.

Defining terrorism is not only a way to prevent certain kinds of illegal activity, but also, through it, Islam is given its own status (especially when discussing "Islamic terrorism"). In the Barcelona process, the states are, in relation to Islamic movements, representatives and guarantors of rightful Islam. The states do not aim to be Islamic actors, but by their political power they define acceptable Islam – that is, an Islam that is non-political, cultural and something belonging to personal religious life. For its own part, the state level wants clearly to de-articulate the relationship between Islam and violence.

State-level Islam is non-political and private. Terrorists represent political and public Islam; they aim to bring forward their interests through the public articulation of Islam. The self-identification of the states in relation to terrorists is constructed through the aspect of legality, and also by positioning Islam. The principle of privatization of Islam gives the state the possibility to narrow strongly the space of the political articulation of Islam.

The otherness articulated through Islam "locates", in relation to terrorism, at national level. In relation to Islamists and other groups that are regarded as terrorists, SEM countries are able to construct their democratic and legal identity, which is also supported by the EU. In the Barcelona process, SEM countries can build their national existence through a transnational context and use it against national-level actors. In the Barcelona process, Islam plays an important part for SEM countries in creating a positive identity because state represents "good" and acceptable Islam, and, in opposition, the non-acceptable Islam is represented by terrorists, which actually is not Islam at all. The right of the state to define the possibilities and forms of the representation of Islam is confirmed in the Barcelona process.

When taking the articulation of Islam and terrorism as a reference, an interesting situation develops regarding the state level between EU and SEM countries. In most cases, the articulation of the threat of Islam has meant, in an appropriate context, juxtaposing Europeans versus non-European Mediterranean countries or, more generally, the north versus the south. The result it that non-European Mediterranean countries have then formed a kind of bloc that appears to be a homogeneous threat to Europe. This division – in which Islam has had an important and negative role – has greatly dominated the discourse between the north and the south.

In putting this into a longer historical timeframe one can see that in the Barcelona process the state level of the EU and SEM countries approach each other *in this regard*. Terrorism is a problem for both: the political activity of Islamists actually provides a common enemy for both the EU and SEM countries, and this enemy is articulated through Islam. Therefore, Islam is not a dividing factor between the northern and southern shores of the Mediterranean; at an official level it is instead a unifying factor. Historically, the situation is peculiar because a certain kind of Islam becomes a common enemy that is used against national actors inside SEM countries.

Thus, various kinds of political activities are broadly defined as terrorism, and that creates a rather contradictory discourse. Is all action against the government random and unfounded terrorism (i.e. violence)? Or can these different "terrorist" groups be partners in constructing a wider perspective for political participation? Islam has an intermediary position here, because through it some things can be deemed non-acceptable. There are violent groups among various political Islamic movements, but not all of them use violence. The discourse that attacks political Islam, and which the Barcelona process and the EU have also intensified, aims to brand all groups as violent and illegitimate movements.

Terrorism, and defining good and bad Islam, is not a way to build bridges across the Mediterranean; rather, it is meddling in domestic affairs. The role of the EU is open to debate: it wants to support the democratic and legal identity of SEM countries, but in practice this means narrowing the democratic rights of national-level actors in those countries.

As a summary we can say that seizing Islam in the Barcelona process is one way of constructing state and national identity; others that potentially control or claim the role of political Islamic identity can be delegitimized through the meaning produced in an international context. The nation's identity is therefore born through, on the one hand, international actions, and, on the other, national actions. An outside force, the European Union, also has a role in constructing this identity. This identity could, in my view, be called *legalistic identity*. It is important to see how, for SEM countries, the otherness of Islam is constructed at a national level (i.e. in relation to national Islamists), rather than in relation to the European Union or the West more generally.

Muslim community in international context

The articulation of Islam through culture and terrorism forms just a small part of the Barcelona process to which can be included several other themes. At first sight, one could say that for SEM countries as a whole, Islam does not consist of any significant source of identity in the Barcelona process. In spite of this, it is obvious that cultural and terrorism-linked articulation of Islam helps, for its own part, to understand the national identities of SEM countries in the context of the Barcelona process. Thus it can be seen that views on Islam within SEM countries and the EU are very similar: culture and terrorism represent the non-political articulation of Islam *in relation to the European Union*.

The form of Muslim community can also be examined at a more general level. Here it is interesting to ask whether one can talk about Muslim community in the Barcelona process. How do we think the Muslim community is construed in relation to the EU, rather than just in relation to terrorists or other national groups or themes? The idea of Islamic *activism* is in close contact with the idea of Islamic communality. The communality and activism made possible by the Barcelona process can be compared and contrasted to one important international Islamic organization: the Organization of Islamic Conference (OIC). This organization is particularly interested in politicizing Islam and constructing Islamic identity.

The basis for founding the OIC was laid in a meeting of the Arab countries in 1969 when they tried to create a common strategy for solving the Middle East crisis and condemning Israel. Co-operation was also extended to cover non-Arab Muslim countries, and the common factor, together with political and economic factors, was the historical bond to Islam. The OIC is seen to serve as a unifying factor for the Muslim world in relevant international questions and to promote the development of Muslim countries and the renaissance of the Muslim culture (Tiukkanen 1994, 215–216, 221). The ideological base of the OIC is to unite the Muslim community, *umma*, in the form of co-operation between states (cf. Al-Ahsan 1988, 13).

Though the main motives behind the OIC are to form both unity and a common policy, it has also provided a signal to the outside world. It can be regarded as a joint political forum for Muslims through which the views of the Muslim world and Islamic politics are reflected. States, and in this case governments, are seen as the producers and manifesters of international Islamic politics. Even if the meaning of the *umma* is emphasized here, the politics linked to Islam are particularly produced by the state-level actors in this context.

Against this background, the Euro-Mediterranean Co-operation can be interpreted as a potential forum for "Islamic" voices. It contains the same actors as in the OIC, and for this reason it is possible to tackle such political matters for which there perhaps would be no other arena. At the same time, one must keep in mind that the Barcelona process was not, from the outset, an Islamic forum and it is not primarily a vehicle for Islamic politics. Rather, it is a question of co-operation between participants who form the majority of the Muslim countries of the region.

The OIC and other potentially Islamic political communities cannot straightforwardly combine politics with Islam or give concrete political doctrines based on Islam. It is more a question of articulating and politicizing the cultural background and, in that way, becoming conscious of a common identity. In the Barcelona process it is interesting to reflect on whether there were any attempts to articulate this unity or bring forward political divisions through it.

The Barcelona process is not a question of implementing a common and unified Islamic policy, because inner contradictions prevent that, even at the level of speeches. Instead, we can talk about communality or the forming of identity. There is no state that is "characteristically" or "by definition" an Islamic one, but that is not the main point here.

The basic question is how these Arab states, whose identity is more or less defined by Islam, articulate their interests potentially through Islam in contexts such as the Barcelona process. The articulation of Islam can then be compared to the case of the OIC, which has the same actors as the Barcelona process. Furthermore, both contexts are mainly secular, meaning that Islam finds only a marginal place in each. This does not, however, mean it will fail to receive a mention now and again.

EU and SEM countries have similar interests in the Barcelona process in those matters in which Islam is articulated in some way (terrorism and cultural affairs). Because of this, the process is quite different from the OIC at the level of Islamic actors; the logic of political actorness and political interests is different. In the OIC, the starting point is to build Islamic communality and act as its own entity. Furthermore, the participators are all Muslim countries. This is not the case in the Barcelona process, where the logic of the process is shown in a different way. In this process, Islam is detached from the actions of Muslim states and touches only some issues – i.e. culture and terrorism. Islam is not, thus, a general reference to action in the Barcelona process as it is in the context of the OIC.

One can say, then, that the performance of the countries regarded as Islamic in the international political arena is in the same way as heterogeneous as any other political activity attached to Islam. This means that there is no definite formula according to which "Islamic" actors would act together in an international context. However, one may question the common features and goals of different contexts.

The relationship between actorness and context comes clearly to the fore in this because different contexts produce a distinctly different outlook, even though the "Islamic" actors would be the same (i.e. state-level actors represented by the highest political elite). In some situations, Islamic politics are clearly visible and are used as a tool. The early phases of the Barcelona process show a situation in which the Islamic element stays clearly in the background (or, at least, does not receive any primary role in the policies of the state-level actors or in forming of identity).

The obvious reason for the lack of an Islamic element is that SEM countries see the Barcelona process mainly as an economic forum, with politics and cultural aspects as secondary elements. One can also say that the state-level actors do not want solely to be the bearers of the Islamic identity, but also of Arab identity, which is combined to secular ideology. The third factor for the limited articulation of Islam is the nature of the process: the actions and goals of EU and SEM countries are united in this process. Thus SEM countries have just a limited possibility to articulate their interests from their own starting points.

Even if Islam is present in the Barcelona process on the level of identification – as the culture and terrorism section indicates – it is an exaggeration to speak about an Islamic community. The Barcelona process gives some elements for constructing this kind of communality. This community is, however, quite "loose" in terms of the articulation of Islam, and therefore it is difficult to consider it as primarily an Islamic community.

NOTES

1 Libya was not allowed to participate. The reason for this was the international boycott because of the bombing of a plane which crashed in Lockerbie, Scotland (see e.g. Khader 1995, 14).
2 Euro-Mediterranean Conference, 1995. See also Progress Report on the Euro-Mediterranean Partnership, 1997 and Conclusions: Second Euro-Mediterranean Ministerial Conference, 1997.
3 See King and Donati (1999, 156) who argue that it was impossible to talk directly about "Muslim fundamentalism" without endangering the whole process. In what way the word "terrorism" is relevant to other extremist political activity, e.g. the movements in Israel, is outside the scope of this study.
4 This is backed up by the statement of the Commission's official, Laurence Auer, in which he said that SEM countries have also been active in bringing terrorism to the Barcelona agenda (interview with Auer, 16 December 1997). In the speeches given in the meeting, terrorism was often mentioned both by EU and SEM countries. See, e.g., the speeches by Klaus Hänsch, president of the European Parliament, and the foreign ministers of Algeria, Tunisia and Turkey (Rede des Präsidenten des Europäischen Parlaments Dr. Klaus Hänsch; Intervention de Monsieur Mohamed Salah Dembri; Discours de Monsieur Habib Ben Yahia, and Statement by Turkey, H.E. Mr. Deniz Baykal).
5 The concept of monopolizing Islam comes from Amira Huweidy (interview with Huweidy, 17 February 1997).

2

The Muslim Brotherhood:
Protest and Politics

Introduction

When we talk about political Islam we usually refer to political movements that are clearly "Islamic" or that have an Islamic ideology. In this respect, the movement under examination, the Egyptian Muslim Brotherhood,[1] represents a typical Islamic political actor and movement. In its history, it has been one of the most powerful Islamic groups in Egypt whose influence has spread beyond its borders. It represents a form of political Islam, which I refer to as *Islamism*.

In the case of the Muslim Brotherhood the articulation of Islam and politics is, in principle, obvious because the Brotherhood aims to act inside the political sector as an Islamic movement. Thus this case represents quite clearly the articulation of Islam in a traditional political context. The Islamic dimension of the Brotherhood is generally accepted both by the movement itself and by outside political actors. In spite of this, an interesting point in the Islamic dimension of the Brotherhood is the manner of articulation.

Earlier, this book examined how Islam is politicized in an international context and how national Islamic identity is constructed. In the case of the Brotherhood the interest is focused on how Islamic politics are integrated into national politics and how the Islamic identity of the movement is formed. The analysis of the role of the Egyptian state is an essential part of this – that is, how the state affects the Islamic politics of the Brotherhood and the construction of identity. The crucial debate here surrounds the possibility of producing Islamic politics both from the ideological and practical point of view.

In this chapter, the analysis is divided in two larger parts. First: there's an examination of the Islamic dimension of the Brotherhood's politics and the composition of identity from the organization's own point of view. The programs of the Brotherhood are studied, through which can be grasped the ideology of the movement. Second: the Brotherhood is compared with other groups in Egypt that represent political Islam one way or another because the construction of the Brotherhood's own Islamic identity can partly be understood through different social connections. Against that background the Brotherhood's own conception of the relationship between Islam and politics is reflected on. By examining these movements the role of the state in the process of the construction of Islamic identity also becomes more clear.

The Muslim Brotherhood is a movement that has a reasonably established organization, membership and activities. As a political actor it differs from many other Islamic organizations whose activities are either more secretive, disorganized or have lesser importance. The ideological emphasis and the practical work of the Muslim Brotherhood have varied quite a lot during the course of its history. This chapter aims not to give a picture of the whole history and development of the Brotherhood but to concentrate predominately on its ideology and political status at the end of the 1980s and during the 1990s.

The history of the Brotherhood and present political status

If political Islam is examined specifically in the form of Islamic groups, the role of Egypt in their development cannot be ignored. Together with Iran, Pakistan and Algeria, Egypt is one of the most important countries to have influenced the form and content of Islamism. The Islamic policy of Egypt has many faces: there are moderate reformers and radical militant movements, not forgetting the "official" Islam. Some of these movements have concentrated on social activities; others are clearly trying to have a say in national politics (Krämer 1996, 210). If Egypt has been one of most pivotal countries affecting Islamism, the Muslim Brotherhood of Egypt is one of the oldest and most important still existing Islamic movements. It was founded by Hassan al-Banna in 1928, and the movement has been an example for many Islamic movements both in Egypt and in other Arab and Muslim countries.[2]

The political and social situation in Egypt has experienced many changes during the Brotherhood's lifespan, which have reflected on the work and principles of the movement. The Brotherhood was born at a time when the caliphate had recently fallen, and colonialism and the influence of a Western lifestyle continued. In addition to these outside factors, the most important forces behind the birth of the Brotherhood were, perhaps, the setbacks of Egypt's modernization project: political, social and economic reforms were not carried through. Historically, the birth of the Brotherhood has been important, but not surprising in the circumstances. An unstable social situation provided a good base for the birth and development of a new mass movement.

The Brotherhood gained broad support relatively quickly and, after World War II, the membership was estimated to be around one million members. The Brotherhood was the first middle-class, urban mass movement in Egypt. Its founder, Hassan al-Banna, emphasized that he intended to guard the interests of the middle class, and the movement's program reflected a respect for work and the idea of national economics (Zdanowski 1988, 49–50).

In the 1952 revolution (a military coup aimed at the overthrow of King Farouk I, the abolition of the constitutional monarchy, and the establishment of a republic) the Brotherhood had a significant role even though "Free officers" were the actual executors. However, the relationship with the new government and the Brotherhood soon became strained and the movement has been banned since 1954. Even if the movement has not had official status, it has been able to operate in politics more or less openly in different times. Nevertheless, in the Abdel Nasser era (1954–1970) the Brotherhood occasionally experienced quite harsh treatment because it was suspected of revolutionary activities. The rule of Anwar Sadat (1970–1981) led to a gradual liberation of the Brotherhood's activities. One turning point was in the 1980s, when the Brotherhood was able to attend the elections – not as an individual group, however, but in coalition with other established parties.[3]

The Brotherhood became an important force in national politics in Egypt in the 1980s. It can be regarded as one of the most important opposition movements at the time, to the point that in the beginning of the 1990s the government thought it to be too powerful. The 1990 elections were seen as protest elections and were boycotted by several parties including the Muslim Brotherhood when the government tried to suppress their activities. The same thing also happened during the 1995 elections.

The Muslim Brotherhood: politicization of Islam and identity

In the Euro-Mediterranean Co-operation, Muslim states were able to define a form of Islam in relation to national actors because they could control the political space and the area of political activity in question. Thus, restricting Islam to "own" use was a sign of the state's authority in relation to other political actors that were potentially "Islamic" – e.g. political Islamic movements. Therefore the political Islamic movements must be separated from the state-governed, official or state-controlled organs. They have a different type of relationship to Islam and politics, and to political processes. Historically, politicization of Islam has not been a road to political power for the Brotherhood; rather, it has basically been a factor that was connected to opposition work and to challenging the regime.

The position and Islamic nature of the Muslim Brotherhood must be examined against the political situation in the individual country and the possibilities it allows. It is a group that has had at least a limited opportunity to take part in the state-level political processes. It is also a religiously colored group whose religiousness is thought to be the reason behind the restrictions to participate in politics. Therefore, religion is a factor that both enhances and restricts political participation and activity. In relation to supporters, it gives legitimacy and supports the identity of the group. In relation to the state, religion provides the opportunity to ban political activity because the state has determined that religion is a non-political affair.

In this context, this chapter examines the political programs of the Brotherhood. These are used to illustrate how the Brotherhood differs from other actors and how it presents its own particularity in relation to others. The aim is not primarily to study how the Brotherhood has succeeded and will succeed in realizing the objectives it has stated in its political programs, but to examine what kind of position Islam is given in these programs – that is, how Islam is articulated in the political programs of the Brotherhood.

Throughout its history, the Brotherhood has tried to define its own ideology through different programs and statements. In the following pages, the programs and statements made in the 1990s will be reviewed. These are the documents that largely direct and justify the present-day Brotherhood's political actions. The documents under review were originally written in Arabic, but they have also been translated into English. Arabic documents are somewhat more numerous than translated ones, but the crucial papers also appear in English.

According to Kamal El-Helbawy, the programs initiated in the 1990s were a result of the intellectual process that had already started inside the Brotherhood in the previous decade.[4] The program papers were a reaction to the social conditions in Egypt; one could say that the texts were in keeping with their time. The Brotherhood's point of view becomes clear in the following:

> The Muslim Brotherhood realize that it is their duty [...] to declare to the public in the clearest and strongest words their own position towards certain issues of great significance, which are the subject of a cross-cultural debate. Thus they issued in 1994 several statements indicating precisely their outspoken view regarding issues such as Shura (Islamic consultation), political pluralism, women rights and so on (Muslim Brotherhood 1995, *Our Testimony*).

From these political programs it is possible to discern two methods through which supporters were being reached. The first is the "What is to be done?" programs. Here, the emphasis is on concrete aims and objectives: it concentrates on action. The other method is the "What values do we consider important?" type writings, which are more general in nature. Their purpose is not to organize concrete political actions, but rather to define their own values and beliefs. Thus, they represent symbolic program writing (Pekonen 1995, 25–32).

The different programs of the Brotherhood can be examined through this division. They are not exclusive approaches, but complementary. This division helps to distinguish the role of Islam in the ideological objectives of the Brotherhood. The examination is divided into these two definitions and the variations between them. The purpose is to look at how these variations manifest themselves in the "amount" of articulation of Islam and politics.

With regards the concrete aims of the Brotherhood, different programs are measured in relation to the axis *action–values*. The crucial point here is to examine the articulation of Islam in these different levels of program writing: is Islam articulated and, if so, in what way? How is identity constructed? How is self understood, and how are relationships to other actors constructed in these programs? Of particular interest is the consideration of whether the demands are "religious", "Islamic" or "political", or some combination of these three. What, in the end, is the Islamic dimension of politics?

Political practice: "What is to be done?"

In the "What is to be done?" type program writing, one tries to define those acts with which a meaningful political system should be built. It is a concrete base on which other objectives are built, and through which political participation is, on the whole, possible. The crucial point is to define how the political system is built, the decision-making structures and the power relations. Those objectives that deal with concrete politics refer to practical and everyday political activities.

The Brotherhood's short-term political goals are expressed in collected form in the *15 principles for agreement.*[5] These objectives were formulated at the beginning of the 1990s, and reflect the political situation in Egypt at that time when the status of the Brotherhood was increasingly under threat. The 15 principles are a reaction to the actions of the Egyptian government that also affected the existence of the Brotherhood. Originally, this program was a personal list of demands made by the Brotherhood's religious leader Mahmud El-Hudaybi, but not long after it was used as an election manifesto within the Brotherhood. Thus, it shows the political standing of the Brotherhood with regards elections. Below are the demands in the program.

1. To confirm unequivocally that the people are the source of all power so that it is not permissible for any one individual, party, group or institution to claim the right to authority, or to continue in power except with the consent of the people.

2. Total commitment to, and respect of, the principle of power exchange through free and fair general elections.

3. To confirm the freedom of personal conviction (religious conviction).

4. To confirm the freedom of establishing religious rites for all the known heavenly religions.

5. To confirm the freedom of opinion and the right to publicise it, and to call peacefully, to it, within the limitations of the moral values of society that are detailed in the first section of the constitution. An important consideration in ensuring the above is the freedom of owning and using the different mass media outlets (television, radio, video tapes and equipment, fax machines, newspapers, magazines, books and newsletters).

6. To confirm the right of forming political parties and that no administrative body should have the right to restrict or stop the application of this right. An independent judicial authority should be the only source in confirming what falls outside the

ideals and standards of society, or that which can be thought of as a rejection of peaceful political participation.

7 To confirm the right to public gatherings, the invitation to them, and participation in them, all within the limitations of public safety, and so long as the usage of violence or arms or the threat of doing so is not included.

8 To confirm the right of peaceful demonstrations.

9 To confirm the importance of representing the people through a parliamentary council elected through a free and fair elections, and for a limited period, after which elections are held again.

10 The right of every citizen (man or woman) to take part in parliamentary elections.

11 The right of every citizen to become a member of parliament through elections.

12 Ensuring the independence of the judicial system at all levels while taking all the necessary steps and laying down all the conditions to ensure that it is safe from any source of fear or manipulation, and that no one is to be tried except by a qualified judge. That all exceptional courts are cancelled, and the jurisdiction of the military courts is restricted to cases involving military crimes and violations only.

13 The separation between the prosecution and investigation authorities, and that the public defence authority should be independent from the minister of justice. Furthermore, whoever it (public defence authority) condemns to imprisonment should have the right of appeal to a judicial authority against that decision.

14 The army must stay clear of politics, concentrating only on protecting the country's external security, and that it should not be used, neither directly nor indirectly, by the governing authority in enforcing its wishes and control, or in prohibiting the people's rights.

15 The police and all other security services must protect the security of the nation and society as a whole, and its utilisation in maintaining the state or as means of crushing opposition opinion should be prohibited. A system that overlooks its work and leadership, and ensures the above, should be imposed. More specifically, it (the security forces) must not be allowed to intervene in political activities and general elections.

These principles focus on guarding the basic rights and follow quite closely the form and content of traditional Western constitutions. They emphasize, among other things, keeping separate executive and judicial power, and the importance of free elections. Many of those demands deal with freedom of expression, freedom of participation and free elections. The Brotherhood bases its list on the constitution and, through that, it tries to legitimate its political participation.

The demands of the Brotherhood are objectives of an opposition movement. With them it tries to ensure the right of political activity in relation to the state. For instance, founding a party should, according to the Brotherhood, be free in the sense that any official organ should not have the power to limit or prohibit this right. This view is supported by the demand that only an independent judicial – not political – authority would have the ability to define which parties are suitable for Egyptian society. The Brotherhood emphasizes the independence of the institutions that deal with enforcing law, criminal investigation and prosecution from political governance. The same applies to the role of the army, the police and other security organs.

The idea of goals and targets expressed in the political program of the Brotherhood contains the inherent idea of enemies in politics and of "otherness". There is no mention of any particular enemies, but the demands are targeted towards organizing practical political activity and structures. The strongest demands deal explicitly with the rights and liberties of citizens in relation to the state and government.

The demands rise from the Brotherhood's own political situation and its definition. As already mentioned, the Brotherhood's rights to participate in political life have been restricted almost throughout its history. From the political program one can read how the Brotherhood wants to have constitutional foundations for its existence. The message is directed at political leadership that has the power to determine the practices of Egypt's political system. The demands for liberties and rights are therefore targeted at those political actors who have the power to implement those demands. In the case of Egypt, it is the executive political leadership, which comprises the president, the ruling party (the National Democratic Party) and the political elite around them.

There is no mention in the Brotherhood's program of the problems of organizing the state's highest governing organs. The reason for this is that the existence of the state is taken for granted. The internal tasks and rights of the state can be defined or "strengthened", but the overall structure is taken as given. This also shows the opposition position of the proposer of the program and the nature of constitutional battle.

Demands are related to the structure of the society inside which there is an intention to strengthen the existing constitutional rights and demand their implementation. There is no attempt in the program to create a new political order, but the existing structure is in many regards thought be good enough.

At surface level, it seems that the role of Islam in these demands is not expressed openly or its role is, at least, a very minor one. The demands for everyday politics are, in a religious sense, neutral and therefore those political demands are not articulated through Islam. Thus, conflictual differentiations are also not undertaken in the form of articulating Islam. Though Islamic movements are often and self-evidently called "religious" or "Islamic", the Islamic nature of the Brotherhood, too, needs to be evaluated: an Islamic dimension is not distinctly articulated in all ideology.

This could be compared to, for instance, Abdel Azim Ramadan's opposing interpretation of the Brotherhood of the 1970s. According to him, the Brotherhood's view on economic, social and political problems was *exclusively* religious. These problems originated from the fact that the Islamic *sharia* was not applied in practice (Ramadan 1993, 166). The view of Ramadan is partially time-bound, but it also expresses how the political programs of Islamic groups are often interpreted: they are seen through religious arguments, which then means that the importance of "purely" political demands are not taken enough into consideration.

In what way, then, does the Brotherhood explain the Islamic content of these demands? They could rather be seen as basic assumptions for a democratic state. In a concrete sense, the program of the Brotherhood does not commit, for example, to religious governance where a religious elite would determine the content of politics. As the spiritual leader at that time, El-Hudaybi, mentions in the ideology of the Brotherhood, the secular and the sacred are two different things. In practice, this suggests that political governance is in the hands of earthly powers, and the religious elite do not have any particular role in it (interview with El-Hudaybi, 3 March 1997).

The political sector belongs, therefore, to the territory of the civil government, but this does not prevent politics from being Islamic at an ideological level. Even if Islam does not find articulation in political demands and objectives, the Brotherhood regards them to be Islamic. According to the Brotherhood, the aforementioned demands and objectives are to be found in Islam defined by the Brotherhood. The basic starting point is the view that the democratic system is part of Islam (interview with El-Hudaybi, 22 February 1997).

This view turns the whole picture upside down: a democratic system is not a separate – just and only – Western political system but it is being "Islamized", i.e. seen as a phenomenon inside Islam. The 15 principles are a way of implementing not only democracy (in a Western sense) as such but also Islam. One can ask, of course, which precedes which (Islam before democracy or democracy before Islam), but that is a meaningless question because one can also assume that the basic assumptions of democracy and Islam do not have to contradict each other. This issue will be discussed later when examining the longer-term goals of the Brotherhood.

Though Islam is not articulated on the level of concrete demands, and other political actors are not classified through Islam, the Brotherhood is willing to think that on the whole the principles are Islamic. Thus the 15 principles are important for self-identification: the demands are one way of defining the self for the Brotherhood through Islam, because those demands represent the essentials of Islam for them. According to this logic the actual target of those demands – the state of Egypt and the ruling elite – is seen as non-Islamic, and the conflictual articulation of self and other occurs through Islam, even though it is not explicitly included in the program text.

As a whole, these 15 principles emphasize political solutions that are based on renewing political practices. Political articulation of Islam does not occur as such and, for an outside observer, there is no clear separation from other political actors through that articulation. Nevertheless, the Brotherhood has other program texts in which the relationship between politics and Islam is more obvious: the articulation of Islam is emphasized and political objectives are further away from the concrete political arena.

The long-term goals: Islamic state and sharia
The 15 principles of the Brotherhood represent most clearly the definition of action – that is, the "What is to be done?" kind of program writing. But, as mentioned earlier, the level of concrete political activity is not the only level on which the programs of the Brotherhood should be examined. When we move on to the more symbolic and value-defining

level, the situation changes. There is a level of program writing in between action and values, and one example of this is the Brotherhood's views on the Islamic state and *sharia*. Implementing the Islamic state and *sharia* is a question of long-term goals; however, realizing those objectives is dependent on short-term actions and changes through them. Therefore they follow each other chronologically.

The political objectives of the Brotherhood culminate in fulfilling the ideas of the Islamic state and *sharia* (the Islamic law). Putting them into practice is the ultimate goal of all activities. However, such goals as the 15 principles are the product of the idea of *sharia*, which means *sharia* has significance even before it is firmly implemented. As the Brotherhood puts it:

> While we hold that the Quran and the Prophet's tradition are the supreme constitution of the rule of Muslims and that anything that is against them cannot be accepted or considered, we see that the nation must have a written constitution that is laid down and agreed upon. Its tenets should be taken from the texts of the *sharia*, and from its goals, objectives and general rules. This constitution should include rules to govern the relationship between the different governmental organizations so that they do not overstep their areas of work. It should also contain sufficient rules and principles to preserve and protect public and private liberties for all people, Muslims and non-Muslims (*A brief note on shura*).

The Islamic state and *sharia* are closely connected. According to El-Hudaybi, implementing the Islamic state is important so that *sharia* would be enforced. The Islamic state and *sharia* are a precondition of each other. The essential point is that *sharia* should be implemented gradually, not like in Iran – that is, through revolution. According to the former leader of the Brotherhood, Muhammad Hamid Abul Nasr, gradual implementation is characteristic for *sharia* (in Ramadan 1993, 176–177). Mustafa Mashhour, the Brotherhood's leader in the 1990s, thinks that gradual development and the idea of change is included in the action of the Prophet Mohammed: when power is pursued in the name of Islam, it does not necessary mean the immediate use of arms (Mashhour in Karawan 1997, 21).

These aspirations mean diverging from concrete political aims. Striving for founding an Islamic state is another kind of objective than the objectives described in the 15 principles. Those principles are attached to day-to-day politics and to improving the existing situation. On a political level, they are the things that, chronologically, should be changed first. The demand for an Islamic state and the implementation of *sharia* are to be realized later and should be implemented through those gradual changes.

From the point of view of gradual change, the participation of the Brotherhood in the parliamentary work at the end of the 1980s and in the beginning of the 1990s has had various implications. Participation has been important in itself because the Brotherhood thinks that political participation should be undertaken through existing channels:

> All their work has been carried out through the legitimate channels and the Muslim Brotherhood has never worked outside the law. It worked through legally recognized insititutions such as parliament, syndicates, academic councils, student unions, etc. (Mashhour 1995, *God is sufficient for us*).

According to the Brotherhood, democracy is a form of government in accordance with the spirit of Islam, and *sharia* is by definition attached to the Islamic form of government. According to the Brotherhood, *sharia*'s implementation was put aside in the last century and the state governed by laws that are not Islamic. Participating in the parliamentary work in the aforementioned period was, for the Brotherhood, a possibility through which it could pursue those politics that would better enhance Islam:

> The Muslim Brotherhood's determination to participate in the parliament is not an aim nor a goal but rather a means to invite the officials to the true remedy (i.e. Islam) instead of seeking it in man-made doctrines (Mashhour 1995, *God is sufficient for us*).

According to El-Hudaybi, the Brotherhood tries to implement the Islamic state using "the democratic way". El-Hudaybi sees this as implying that the Islamic state cannot be created unless people want it or believe in it. This idea cannot, therefore, be *enforced* on people (interview with El-Hudaybi, 22 February 1997). In order to verify support, a political system with democratic and free elections needs to exist. The Brotherhood submits itself, thus, to a parliamentary process.

The demands to implement *sharia* have also been criticized. Opponents of the Brotherhood say that Egypt's legislation is much like *sharia* even now. When questioned about the situation in Egypt in implementing *sharia*, El-Hudaybi answered:

> This is sophistry! For it is incumbent upon the ruler from the outset to promulgate laws which conform to the *sharia* and not to obstruct the command of God (interview in 1987, El-Hubaybi in Ramadan 1993, 178).

There is a multitude of interpretations in implementing *sharia*. Though usually people agree on the meaningfulness of *sharia*, there is no unanimity on its implementation or even on its meaning. Some think that *sharia* mainly gives general ethical advice and that it has nothing to do with politics or arranging social relations. To others, however, it means merely a cultural reference on which the legislature should more or less rely on. Another extreme is to think that *sharia* should cover all human life and existence (see e.g. Botiveau 1993, 264; Najjar 1992, 68 and Shepard 1996). For the Brotherhood, *sharia* means an ideological and religious objective that determines practical actions. The objective is very idealistic and is hard to reach; it is equally as hard to define its contents. Nevertheless, that is the final objective of political activity, and it makes the Brotherhood an Islamic group.

For Islamic politics, the demand for an Islamic state is productive because it is, in principle, unattainable. When trying to achieve the ideal of an Islamic state, individual political work must always be related to that. Productivity is created by the fact that the unattainability of the objective gives a reason and possibility to undertake politics and political divisions. The question is whether the Islamic state is estimated to be here, and now, or at some point in the future. If it exists already, then Islam cannot be used in the same way as a political factor, because all the other political actors would also be Islamic actors. The Brotherhood thinks that the Islamic state will be born in the future, and that makes it possible to ideologize and politicize Islam. Even though there would be no clear definitions of an Islamic state and it would seem to be something like the "Western" democratic model, the politicization of Islam would give a direction and identity base for undertaking politics.

Shifting from short-term goals to longer-term objectives means that the articulation linked to Islam would increase, moving chronologically and ideologically to another level. The Brotherhood would distance itself from those concrete proposals according to which political life should be organized. Nevertheless, it would still act in the political sector but on a broader scale. In this connection, the lesser details are not discussed (as in the 15 principles) but the focus is on organizing society in a more general level, society as a whole, where the objective is the founding of an Islamic state and the implementation of *sharia*.

The demands for an Islamic state and *sharia* are directed at non-Muslims and to those (secular) Muslims who do not hold these demands as a basis for political action. Implementation of *sharia* and an Islamic state means that political divisions would be made more clearly through articulation based on Islam, as was the case in the 15 principles. There is, however, a certain paradox if *sharia* and an Islamic state are to be realized based on the thinking of the Brotherhood. The form of government they strive for (the Brotherhood calls it "democracy") is hard to link specifically and explicitly to Islam. But, of course, *sharia* in itself, by mere implementation, carries the meanings attached to Islam.

In any case, the political divisions appear in the texts of the Brotherhood according to who wants to implement the program objectives and who does not. In that sense, it can be said that Islam is the form of articulating differences; the distinctions both from the existing and ruling political actors and at a more general level from the actors opposing the Islamic form of government is undertaken through Islam. This way the actors' identities in relation to Islam will be defined.

The political dimension of values: women's role

The programs mentioned previously are connected to political activity that occurs in the sector of politics. When we move towards the values in the action–value axis, the aspectual nature of politics becomes clearer. At this point, politicality is no longer just about firm aims or sectoral–political activities, but also a general attitude to different things, from which one can draw conclusions about the important values of the Brotherhood. Then, also, Islam receives a clearly articulated form.

How, from this point, does the Brotherhood make itself distinct from other political actors so that Islam can be clearly articulated? When we examine the programs and statements of the Brotherhood in different fields, Islam is often linked to, for example, the woman's role, family and morality. The following text examines more closely the role of women in the statements of the Brotherhood and its meaning for identity and in politicizing Islam.

Examination of women's role is not a theme chosen randomly. It forms a significant part of the existence and ideology of Islamic movements. Gudrun Krämer, when talking about the core of Islamic activities, mentions the woman's role along with *sharia* (Krämer 1996, 215). Thus, the essential concept of Islam, *sharia*, is equated with a characteristically non-Islamic thing that has, however, importance when we examine the articulation of Islam in a society. With the discourse connected to women we can define borders between both Muslim and non-Muslim communities and between a genuine Muslim community and the "inner otherness" (Eickelman and Piscatori 1996, 89).

The role of women in Egyptian society has experienced changes during recent decades. According to Hala Shukrallah, the reason has been the ongoing modernization process and the ensuing construction of a secular state which has effected the widening of the woman's role and the entering of women into public life. Reduced religious control in society and the growth of secular institutions has made possible women's increasing participation in the functions of society. Islamic movements have been a reaction to this kind of development where tradition and the authentic cultural forms have been under threat (Shukrallah 1994, 26).

At the beginning of the 1990s, the Brotherhood formulated a separate program for the role of Muslim women in an Islamic society.[6] In that program the role and importance of women as mother, child, sister and wife is emphasized. Women are said to comprise the other half of society and are responsible for the "upbringing, guiding and renewing of the continuous generations of men and women. Woman is the one who anchors the principles and faith into the souls of the nation" (Muslim Brotherhood, *The role of Muslim women*).

In a religious sense, women have exactly the same responsibilities as men, and a woman is "accountable" in her faith only to God. The Brotherhood makes itself distant from interpretations that question the religious purity of women:

> There is no direct or indirect text in the Islamic law [*sharia*] that even remotely suggests that women are inherently evil or impure as found in some distorted creeds (Muslim Brotherhood, *The role of Muslim women*).

Women mainly have the same opportunities to participate in public life as men. Women can vote and be elected to parliament and other representational or administrational organs. The only exception to this, according to the Brotherhood, is the office of president, which is thought to be an impossible position for women.

In defining concrete political goals, the Brotherhood does not much refer to traditional sources of Islamic law. Articulation is undertaken by other means: resorting to the constitution or relating to the political situation. Things are different when it comes to the role of women.

According to the program, a woman's life can largely be articulated by referring to different doctrines. In the program text there are, among other things, instructions for women's political, economic, and religious duties and rights and also those attached to family. Almost without exception they refer to the Quran, *hadith* or other authorized sources when there is a need to justify something. This approach can be described as an *authority rhetoric* (Palonen 1997, 37) – that is, they appeal to factors outside of the existing social sphere such as religious dogma. Justifications for demands are rarely taken from social or political spheres as was done in the 15 principles.

It is also interesting that the meaning of historical tradition is more obvious here than in the case of political demands. Women are situated in a historical continuity that goes back as far as the mother and wife of the Prophet Mohammed and to other women of his time:

> It has been shown throughout the history of Islam that women took part in the First and Second Ba'yat al-Aqabah (pledges of allegiance). Furthermore, it was Khadija, the wife of the Prophet Mohamed (SAAS) who was the first to believe in, support and comfort our Prophet. It was Somayya who was among the first to be martyred upholding Islam (Muslim Brotherhood, *The role of Muslim women*).

How does one build political borders and allies in this kind of situation? How is otherness constructed? First of all, one can examine why this program declaration is undertaken, and to whom it is directed. The declaration appears to be moderate and emphasizes the importance of women. Thus, it can be interpreted that the Brotherhood tries to separate itself from the harder-line Islamists whose view on the role of women is clearly more conservative. Moderate politics and the publishing of the program serve other functions, too. They are a way of showing the progressive nature of the organization to possible supporters and to some degree to Western countries or other Western actors that could be potential supporters of the Brotherhood.

The second separating factor is the way in which the position of women is articulated. Since articulation is undertaken by relying on Islamic doctrines, it is also a source of division. However, emphasizing Islam means that those who are not religious but secular are separated by default. A woman's position and importance arises from Islam, and therefore a non-believer in a Muslim society inevitably has a different interpretation of this. On the other hand, other Muslims' views may also deviate from the Brotherhood's, and then it is also a separating factor between Muslims.

What implications, then, do these different interpretations have on social life? The answer is linked to the concretizing of Islam as defined by the Brotherhood. In sectoral–political programs, Islam is not really articulated and is replaced by "realpolitik" arguments in which the liberties, responsibilities and possibilities of a citizen are not derived from the religious sources, but their nature is clearly judicial and they are situated in the logic of the structures of a democratic state.

In defining a woman's role, the arguments go deeper into the doctrines of Islam and history than was the case in the 15 principles and in demands to establish an Islamic state. A woman's role is defined in many different ways that are connected to the early days of Islam and to different periods of history: that role is articulated, first, through the doctrine of Islam, and second, through the narratives attached to Islam. At the same time, a broader concept of Islam as a whole is given. It is not just a question of a woman's role but of Islam in a broader sense, and therefore it is also important in constructing identity. In that definition the idea of Islam is articulated, and at the same time a position towards other Muslims is built, not so much towards the state or certain political groups.

The well-defined articulation of a woman's role through Islam is partly linked to the historical development of Muslim countries. For instance, in the Muslim countries of the Middle East social conditions have changed quite a lot during the centuries, and therefore organizing political life according to the model of the Prophet Mohammed is difficult even in practice. The articulation of family (and through it the roles of men and women) in an Islamic way has not changed much in the majority of Muslim countries both in a legal and cultural sense. Even if an Islamic political and economic system is hard to define, things related to family, sex and women can be determined quite accurately – although not without contradictions (Ayubi 1995, 84, 89).

The role of women is a central moral and ethical sphere of life in which the borders and contents of collective and public Islam are defined. The Brotherhood follows the Islamic idea that morality and ethics belong to the public and collective sphere, not to a private individual. By defining the role of women the Brotherhood can place itself in the public arena so that the Islamic dimension will become explicitly articulated. In this process it rests especially on Islam's collective – not individual – concept of relationship between the individual and society.

To the Brotherhood (and other Islamic movements), the political arena does not provide the possibility of responding to state actions, but the public space (to which morality, family, the role of women and sex belong) is a channel through which the Brotherhood can express its own Islamic dimension in a political sense. The program concerning the role of women is one way of bringing the theme of women to a public debate and submitting it for publicity and confrontation: women's role is thus politicized.

All in all, it could be said that the role of women is essential to the Brotherhood's Islamic identity. Even though the Brotherhood's general attitude towards women is relatively tolerant, the private and public representation of women has an important role. Here the Brotherhood resembles many other Islamic organizations for which women especially are the bearers of authentic Islamic values and Islamic identity. With the help of women the boundaries of the community can be, in some ways, defined to the outside world.

In defining the role of women, Islamic doctrine has its own important role. Through that doctrine moral and ethical starting points are determined. These types of programs are directed at everyone, and through Islam they try to deal universally with different themes. Such a program is also a medium for distancing oneself from political opponents whose Islamic dimension is not articulated in the same way or perhaps not at all.

Islamic dimension in the politics of the Brotherhood

Examining the different program writings of the Brotherhood in the action–values axis, naturally reveals clear differences. Here, those differences were examined solely through the articulation of Islam. But how can one interpret or explain the differences of various program levels? This can be reflected through the Brotherhood's own concept of Islam.[7] The interpretation of Islam is seen as a three-level model where the things related to religious and social life are parallel, rather than mutually exclusive.

The first level comprises the basic principles of Islam: how to execute religious rites and the general ideas of Islam. According to Kamal El-Helbawy, those principles are mainly based on the Quran, which defines *what* to do. This is complemented by *hadith*s, which define *how* certain things should be done. Generally it is question of clear religious duties, not so much of sociopolitical themes (interview with El-Helbawy, 5 December 1997). This level consists of things that are seen as immutable. They are doctrines of Islam that are common to everyone and of which there is a general agreement among Muslims. This part is also quite narrow because there are relatively few clearly defined religious duties in the Quran.

The second level is more open. It is based on rules for which some flexibility of interpretation and change is included. These texts are not as determinate as the Quran or the most important texts in the *hadith*s, the interpretation of which is quite limited. Thus, the possibility of interpretation is greater than in the first level.

The third level goes even further in its openness of interpretation and is wider in scope than the previous two. On this level, there are numerous principles that rise from Islam that have not been defined in detail. More detailed definitions will be determined in a respective situation. This gives leeway to rather a free interpretation of certain things, and therefore there is room, in principle, for new kinds of innovation and action. According to El-Helbawy, one can talk about *consultation* where the content of something or the way of doing it is defined. Consultation can be applied to many different areas in social life, but not to the central religious themes that are strictly defined (interview with El-Helbawy, 5 December 1997).

This three-level model shows the structure of the Brotherhood's thinking. There are a few unambiguous things that are clearly related to

Islam and its doctrine, but things needing interpretation form the major part. The latter category forms the foundation of Islamic politics and action, where it is possible, in principle, to ponder different options both inside the Brotherhood and in society in general.

According to Kamal El-Helbawy, the Brotherhood is not, in its doctrines, tightly attached to any school of thinking; rather, it takes elements from different schools and doctrinal traditions. The Brotherhood tries to formulate its own view of Islam, and thus it differs from many other groups. El-Helbawy criticizes, for instance, the Taleban group in Afghanistan that rigidly follows only certain doctrinal schools and does not seek a doctrinal reform (interview with El-Helbawy, 5 December 1997).

In relation to other levels, the broader level of consultation could be called a place for discussions, negotiations and compromises where suitable Islamic policy for different periods is created. This means that, in essence, the doctrinal structure of the Brotherhood gives room for open Islamic politics. However, it must be noted that the question of "genuine" Islam is left at least partially open: who can say or determine whether the politics of a certain time is Islamic or whether its own interpretations are the only "genuine" options?

The three levels also show ways of articulation that can be recognized as Islamic. At the first level, ideas can easily be recognized as Islamic because references to the Quran or other authoritative sources are direct and quite indisputable or otherwise commonly acknowledged. At the third level, Islam is not discussed in a way that could be recognized unambiguously. Islam is not, therefore, a clearly perceived way of articulation.

In all, this implies in my view that the Brotherhood's articulation of politics through Islam does not give a clear answer to the questions raised by a concrete political situation. Therefore, Islam is not articulated much in the programs directed to the political sector. But if we look at the politics in an aspectual way (i.e. when politics is not just undertaken in the political sector) we can find a possible political articulation of Islam. To put it simply, one could say that the clearer the demands the Brotherhood makes in a political arena (for example, its 15 principles), the less Islamic the articulation, and vice versa: the better something has been able to be articulated through Islam (for example, the definition of women's role), the less it is linked to the building of a political system.

According to the views of the Brotherhood, it is still a question of Islam and executing it. When the organization demands, for example, a democratic and decentralized form of government, it is not following the Western democratic models. The Brotherhood sees it as implementing the *idea* of an Islamic political model: democratic principles are taken from *sharia*. The democratic system is seen as Islamic and therefore it is reasonable to demand such a system in the Egyptian context, too. The question is not whether this kind of a political model can be directly discerned in the religious doctrines; rather, it is that in Islam there is seen to exist a political model corresponding to democracy, and that model should be implemented in the best possible way.

The political system works on a collective level but it does not exist without individuals. In the Brotherhood's thinking, individual and social levels are closely connected. From that point, building the society starts with an individual: the foundation for a good society is to educate individuals together with families. The long-term political reform of the Brotherhood is therefore not possible without first educating individuals to become good Muslims (interview with El-Helbawy, 5 December 1997). The individual and the collective level of politics are thus not separate because the Islamic dimension of an individual is also connected to the Islam of the collective.

El-Helbawy's statement refers to this meaning of the individual's being in relation to his or her actions: "If you are a good Muslim, then you are a good builder" (interview with El-Helbawy, 5 December 1997). The moral values of an individual are transferred into the actions of individuals. Thus, political action is not just about founding a specific Islamic state or implementing *sharia*. The objectives are internally empty if there is not a good Muslim behind them.

One can say, then, that even if the Islamic politics of the Brotherhood does not seem to be credible – that is, Islam is clearly not articulated into politics – it does not mean it would not have importance in some other ways. Here it moves on to the symbolic level of politics, and in this case the birth of Islamic identity can be better understood. Islamic politics proposed by the Brotherhood is very open to well-substantiated counter-arguments and different views; for many, it is also beyond belief, too.

The Brotherhood's political position is, nevertheless, meaningful for the identity of politics. It makes possible the building of self-understanding, and through them one can also define relations to outside political forces. The enabling of the creation of identity is not just about rational and logical options, but also about credible options for a collective in question.

The Islamic dimension of a political system is built on the conflictual articulation of Islam which entails different methods of self-identification. The credibility of Islamic politics does not come from its inner convincing or realizable contents, but expressly from the credibility that is linked to identification; whether it can be regarded as "Islamic". From the Brotherhood's own point of view, the identity of the movement is clearly Islamic. It implements Islam, and the politics and social life is totally based on Islamic principles. The Brotherhood's identity can be regarded as Islamic, but the situation is more complicated when it comes to politicizing Islam because conflictual articulation is not unequivocally based on Islam.

The Muslim Brotherhood and Islamic politics in Egypt

The ideology of the Muslim Brotherhood, how it could be interpreted through different programs, and how it relates to Islam and Egypt's political climate has already been examined. The interesting question arising from this is how the Brotherhood, from its own starting points, can produce its own political identity and, moreover, how it becomes a part of the whole of Egyptian society.

In the case of the Brotherhood, the articulation of Islam follows a logic that makes the organization unique and different in relation to other "Islamic" organizations. These differences, compared to other sorts of Islamic politics, are examined in the following pages. How are these political groups attached to a certain kind of Islam, and what relation do these articulations have with the articulations produced by the Brotherhood? In what way is the Islamic identity of the Brotherhood constructed in relation to these other Islamic groups?

Three kinds of movement are examined here. These chosen movements represent different forms of political Islam, and they at least have something in common with the Brotherhood. That said, their basic principles differ from those of the Brotherhood. On the one hand, these movements show various manifestations of Islamic politics; on the other hand, they reflect the political climate in Egypt in relation to Islamic politics in the 1980s and the 1990s.

There were different phases during those years, and the first one can be described as an Islamic turn of politics in the 1980s when it became possible for Islamic movements to participate in state-level national politics in Egypt. This phase is most obvious in the increasing importance of the Labor Party. At the turn of the decade, obstacles appeared to the participation of certain groups, and this was followed by a hardening attitude of the Islamic movements. Typical during this phase was the rise of Islamic militancy in the social life of Egypt. Since the middle of the 1990s, militant activity and the discourse attached to it has subsided slightly, and parallel to it has come the phase of de-Islamization of politics. This phase is represented here by an organization called al-Wasat.

The politicization of Islam: the Labor Party

Throughout the 1980s, the state of Egypt took a negative view of Islam or, rather, on the existence of Islamic groups in the political sector. The state saw that Islam represented the personal sphere of individuals and it was not desirable to connect it to the political sector. This attitude could also be seen in Egypt's 1977 law on political parties according to which founding a religiously based party was not allowed (see e.g. Sadiki 1995, 262). However, the ban was implemented in a contradictory way because, for example, the activities of the Brotherhood were not totally banned in a legal sense and the organization was allowed to be active, depending on the time period.

Despite the ban on religious political parties in the 1980s, the Islamization of Egyptian politics was obvious. This could be detected, for example, in increasing Islamic rhetoric in public debate when different themes began to be articulated through Islam. Politics articulated in an Islamic way also gained more support in elections. The changing situation in the latter half of the 1980s provided opportunities for political participation for traditional Islamic movements like the Brotherhood as well as for non-Islamic parties whose ideological position contained Islamic elements. An example of such a "re-Islamization" of activities and ideology might be the Islamization of the politics of the Labor Party.

The beginnings of the Labor Party go back to the 1930s when a party called Young Egypt was founded. In those early ideologies, the focus was on opposing imperialism. Adapting socialist economic doctrines was one way of fighting imperialism. The principles of the party were not completely typical of socialist party doctrines, but they were an original combination of social and spiritual aspects (Singer 1993, 7–9).

The first stages of the party were difficult for the Brotherhood. After Nasser's revolution in 1953, the party – then called the Socialist Party – was banned. During Sadat's reign the party was revived at the same time as other opposition parties (Singer 1993, 11). The members of the Labor Party consisted, particularly in those early days, of very many kinds of people. There were, among others, Nasserists, socialists and radical nationalists. However, the party had no organized structure and it was not a major political force in itself (Makram-Ebeid 1996, 124).

During the 1980s, relationships between Islamic movements and the state drew closer in what has been called adjustment or social contract (Meijer 1996, 20). Even though those terms give too bright a picture of the reality, they still tell us about a certain rapprochement between Islamic forces and the state. At exactly that time, the Muslim Brotherhood gained a foothold in politics. First, it made an alliance in 1984 with the secular New Wafd Party, then in the 1987 elections it formed an Islamic Alliance with the Labor and Liberal Parties. At the end of the 1980s, this alliance had become the most important opposition faction in Egypt (Auda 1991, 114).

Joining the alliance was, for the Labor Party, a part of the process where its ideology was Islamized, and where political objectives began to articulate through Islam. For this book, the important point is how the ideology of the Labor Party was shaping up with regard to Islam and socialism. The socialist guidelines of the party were, and still are, distinctly adapted to the Egyptian context and they differed in many respects from those of the European socialist movements. The aspect of nationalism and Arab unity has been strongly present in the guidelines of the Labor Party, as has the idea of social equality (cf. Makram-Ebeid 1989, 427 and Auda 1991, 113–114).

Islam has always been present in some way in the party's ideology. Finding the equilibrium between Islamic and socialist ideas has not been easy inside the party and the balancing act has continued since the foundation of Young Egypt. The debate persisted even after the party was unbanned. Mamoun Fandy analyzes the ideological changes through the ideologist of the party, Adel Hussein. According to Fandy, for a long time Hussein was known for his commitment to Marxism and a Marxist analysis of local problems. The transition from Marxism to

Islamism was not difficult because Hussein's political agenda did not significantly change. Central themes such as social equality, the corruption in the government and Arab unity, continued to have slightly less emphasis. In Hussein's view, the communists had distanced themselves from an important source of ideological justification in putting Islam and Marxism against each other. In practice, the transition to politics articulated in an Islamic sense meant the division of the party into two separate camps: those who supported Islam and those who supported communism. Additionally, there were others who were alienated from the party (Fandy 1993, see also Makram-Ebeid 1996, 124; Utvik 1993, 205 and Singer 1993, 15–30).

Another important phase was the end of the 1980s, when socialist and Islamic groups tried to define the contents of the party's ideology in relation to the themes mentioned above (Singer 1993, 15–30). During this period the emphasis increasingly moved towards Islam. Even though everyone in the party recognized the importance of Islam, "Islamization" received a lot of criticism from those who did not want Islam to have so much weight. There was a fear that "a social democratic party with Islamic roots would become totally Islamic" (Singer 1993, 21–23). The role of Islam in the ideology of the Labor Party has been justified by its "naturalness". Even the socialism of the party was derived from religious values and concepts (see e.g. Singer 1993, 61).

The essential point in this debate is that it took place at all. It shows that the party has distinct and separate options in directing its ideology. Even though Islamic roots were emphasized throughout, Islamism was not a self-evident option for the basis of the party's ideology. It was born as a result of the party's internal processes and therefore other kinds of options would also have been possible. Participation in the Islamic Alliance strengthened the role of religion, and that created a distance from other opposition groups (Singer 1993, 61).

The comparison of relationships with Islam between the Muslim Brotherhood and the Labor Party allows us to understand the Brotherhood's Islamic politics. The Brotherhood began as an Islamic movement. The Labor Party, however, was initially a Marxist movement whose change of ideology towards Islamism was clearly based on political realism. The Islamic dimension of the Labor Party is not so much an in-built quality as it is for the Muslim Brotherhood. It is hard to imagine that a similar debate could have occurred, or would occur, inside the

Brotherhood. Of course, the internal emphasis of the Brotherhood has been prone to change, but it is not likely that the Brotherhood will start to discuss the basis of its ideology like the Labor Party did. The identity of the Brotherhood is more distinctly based on Islam, and it has no other major source of identity.

The Labor Party has been more flexible in its relationship with Islam than the Brotherhood. The Labor Party has been able, at least to some level, to change its identity and the "degree" of politicizing or emphasizing Islam depending on the political tendencies. This shows how articulation is non-essential; the political actor undertakes the articulation in a context, not for necessity. The Labor Party's attitude towards Islam shows itself, for instance, in its relation to implementing *sharia*. According to the party, Islam gives general moral principles and guidelines but does not seek to find any answers for rules and regulations from Islam (see Utvik 1993, 206–207). For the Brotherhood, however, implementing *sharia* is the most important principle directing the work of the party.

The flexibility of Islamization is a significant feature also in relation to other political actors, particularly to the state elite, whose interpretations can change dramatically over time. In part because of this, the Labor Party has been able to act more freely than the Brotherhood in Egyptian political life. The Labor Party has been capable of changing its ideology in order to attain political benefits, but the situation of the Brotherhood has been more difficult. The Labor Party has succeeded in moving flexibly in its articulation of Islam. The proletarian background has probably helped because the party can always revert to those roots.

The Islamic dimension creates for the Labor Party the possibility of changing its identity and therefore it can distance itself from Islam when required without losing political credibility. On the other hand, for the Labor Party the ability to participate in politics is also – in spite of its Islamic tendencies – dependent on the legal status of the party. The party has an official status – that is, it has permission to function as a party, which Islamic movements do not have. This gives the Labor Party a larger leeway than Islamists to express political aims, including those articulated in an Islamic sense.

The political articulation of Islam of the Muslim Brotherhood is more stable than that of the Labor Party. Even though it is sometimes difficult to find any clear articulation of Islam from the political program of the Brotherhood, it is, however, more dependent on it. The Brotherhood can only partially define its own identity: the Islamism of the movement is defined also from the outside. The importance of the Brotherhood's Islamism changes with each political situation, but the movement does not have the same kind of room for maneuver in relation to Islam as the Labor Party.

One example of the constrained relations of the Brotherhood and the state was the exclusion of the Brotherhood from the so-called National Dialogue. The National Dialogue refers to a conference organized in 1994 where, under the leadership of President Mubarak, different political actors were persuaded to come to the same negotiating table in order to tackle the political problems of Egypt. However, there were limitations on who could participate in this dialogue, and the Brotherhood was not given a seat at the table. The participators came mainly from the ruling National Democratic Party (NDP). Opposition forces were represented by the small Tagammu Party and the Labor Party. Even though these movements also strongly criticized the composition and working methods of the dialogue, it is interesting that the Labor Party was included in the dialogue. All the traditional Islamic groups were omitted.

The participation of the Labor Party is significant because it was not seen as an Islamic group; if that had been the case, it would probably have been left out. The party was seen through its legal position, not through its Islamism. This is one example of how the identity of a party is also flexible in the eyes of state authorities and is not based solely on definition coming from Islam. According to David Butter, there were signs at that time that the Labor Party was returning to its roots – that is, to a working class ideology (Butter 1994, 10). Nevertheless, this estimate was premature. Even if the invitation of the Labor Party to the dialogue was seen as an attempt to sever ties between the Brotherhood and the Labor Party, the Islamic tendency of the Labor Party had not disappeared, and the relationship between those two organizations had not been cut (Meijer 1996, 23–24 and interview with Kamal El-Helbawy, 18 December 1998).

The most active and public phase in the co-operation of the Brotherhood and the Labor Party at the end of the 1990s was a sign of the warming up of the relationship between the state and the Islamic movements. The conscious politicization of Islam especially was put in place by the Labor Party to exploit the political climate of that time.

The alliance of the Brotherhood and the Labor Party was, thus, quite a natural development. Both were opposition parties which desired more supporters and a greater foothold in national politics. Many of the concrete goals were common to both parties and they saw each other as a useful tool in order to reach those goals. It was not a question of merging the movements, but rather an electoral move and strategic choice.

Nevertheless, there are common factors in the ideologies of the Brotherhood and the Labor Party, and an Islamic element is one of the most essential. As a whole, however, one can say that the identities of these groups are constructed in different ways. The Brotherhood's relationship with Islam is more clearly articulated and structured. Moreover, it has developed over a long period of time. It is not so vulnerable to changes as is the identity of the Labor Party, where historically the role of Islam had not been very central. Of course, Islam has been one of the most essential sources of identity throughout the Labor Party's entire history, but the direct politicization of Islam has varied rather strongly.

The relatively good political success of the Islamic front at the end of the 1980s did not continue throughout the 1990s. The government's soft policy towards Islamic movements also changed. As a protest against the political situation in Egypt, the major opposition parties – the Muslim Brotherhood, the Labor Party, Wafd and the Liberal Party – boycotted the 1990 elections. Since that time, Islamic groups have had no real possibility of working politically in Egypt. Mamoun Fandy described the situation in a realistic but pessimistic way when he stated: "[T]he political journey of the Islamists and their hope to work within the system to get their share of power seemed to have reached a dead end" (Fandy 1993, 30).

Violence and Islam: the militant Islamic movements

The 1980s was a favorable decade for Islamic politics but the political situation has become increasingly tense since then. Restrictions on political activity and participation were put in place, and the grip of the state and the ruling government on the social processes tightened. For Islamic politics this meant, in practice, banning political activity. Since 1995, the government has striven to destroy the organizational structure of the Brotherhood through repeated incarcerations and military courts, and by severing ties between the Labor Party and the Brotherhood (Meijer 1996, 23).

The harsher tactics of the government did not mean, though, that the Islamic movements would have chosen to curtail their activities; it was more that circumstances forced them to change methods. On the one hand, this meant that some of the Islamic movements went "underground" and kept a low profile. On the other, the tightened social situations meant increasing violent Islamic activity, which led to open confrontations. The battle between militants and the government colored the debate on political Islam at that time, which also had implications on the work and existence of the Brotherhood.

By militant Islamic groups, I mean such Egyptian groups that tried to influence the politics of the country by using armed and other violent methods, and which did not even try to deny those activities (see e.g. Mubarak 1997, 321). Hence, these groups articulated their political demands in the form of violence and totally rejected the existing social and political systems. According to Ibrahim Karawan, they strove to be in a war with the government until it had been overthrown (Karawan 1997, 19).

The most powerful militant groups are Al-Jihad and Al-Jamaʾa al-Islamia.[8] These groups have been responsible for the violence targeted at tourists, the murder of Anwar Sadat in the 1980s, and various other deaths (more in e.g. Ramadan 1993). The mid-1990s was a relatively peaceful period, but at the end of 1997 the situation once again became critical after two large tourist massacres.

The Muslim Brotherhood's own relationship with violence has fluctuated throughout its history. In its early ideology, it supported violence quite openly. The Brotherhood's secret organization of the early days used and supported violent measures. For example, the major ideologist of the movement in the 1950s and the 1960s, Sayyed Qutb, did not rule out violence from political work. The movement has had connections and open co-operation with militant Islamists (see Youssef 1985, 78–84).

The Brotherhood's attitude to violence changed at the end of the 1970s. One factor in this culmination was the Camp David agreement between Egypt and Israel which was strictly condemned by many of Egypt's opposing forces. The Brotherhood's attitude was quite critical but it decided anyway against the use of violence (see Ramadan 1993, 168). The present-day Brotherhood has taken a clearly negative stance on violence. Both in political programs and in its work, the Brotherhood has tried to emphasize its non-violent policy (see e.g. the Brotherhood's program papers *Our Testimony* and *Violence*). Despite accusations, the use and promoting of violence by the Brotherhood has not been proven (see e.g. Human Rights Watch 1997, 276, 278).

The Egyptian government's stand on militant Islamists is clear. They are regarded as major political opponents and attempts have been made to suppress their activities through every possible means. The strategy of the government has been to define opponents as militant terrorist groups, and since 1981 their activities have been suppressed with the aid of a continuous state of emergency. These groups have been completely shut out of the political processes.

The government's relation to Islamists (both militants and moderates) has undergone change. The previous policy tried to distinguish different groups from one another and treat each of them separately. This way, the government could play different groups against each other or combine them against other political enemies, such as Nasserians or communists (Ramadan 1993, 170). This policy, however, has been advantageous for those movements because they have themselves been able to define their relationship towards the state.

The situation changed in the 1990s with the introduction of a common policy. This did not much change the militants' position because negative policy just reinforced the existing situation. That said, the government's policy did have an effect on non-militant Islamic groups and thus on the existence of the Brotherhood. Those groups, which could be called moderates, lost, at least partially, their special status in the eyes of the state. In June 1994, the Brotherhood received a clear message when the prime minister declared the Muslim Brotherhood to be "terrorists" (Kepel 1995, 117). President Mubarak stated also that "violence has always been an essential part" of the Brotherhood's policy, and the Brotherhood cannot be separated from other terrorist groups (see Ayalon 1997, 253, 254).

The government's policy gives to the Brotherhood little room for maneuver because it is treated in the same way as other Islamic movements, including militant ones. This is somewhat controversial because the Brotherhood has tried to distance itself from violent movements. The alliance with New Wafd and participation in the 1984 elections meant dissociating from militant Islamists, which those groups also duly registered. For example, the Jama'a saw the Brotherhood's participation in the elections as "a great sin and insult". In their opinion, the work of the parliament was based on civil laws and therefore it could not pass Islamic laws (Ramadan 1993, 162).

There have been various speculations concerning potential co-operation between different Islamic groups. The Brotherhood has, in some cases, been seen as a potential ally of militant groups but mutual prejudices and reluctance has been obvious. The statement of the leader of Jama'a, Tal'at Fu'ad Qasim, illustrates the position with the Brotherhood:

> We have defined general areas where we can co-operate with other Islamic groups. [...] Our disagreements with the Brothers prevent co-operation. We think that multiplicity and variety are useful as long as the Islamic state has not yet come about (Qasim interviewed by Hisham Mubarak 1997, 317).

The activities and existence of militant Muslims have had an effect on the identity of the Brotherhood in two ways at least. First, the Brotherhood has defined its own identity with regard to violence, and has publicly refuted all use of violence. Second, the violent Islamic movements have influenced the state's attitude towards the Brotherhood, which has had direct implications for its political work. The situation is paradoxical: even if the Brotherhood's connections to militants were almost non-existent and the Brotherhood did not use violence, its role is defined by the state to be just the opposite. It could be said of the similarities with the Brotherhood and militant Islamists that their political Islamic rhetoric is, in some sense, similar but it can be questioned whether there is sufficient ground to treat them as the same kind of movement.

The meaning of terrorism and violence is significant for Egypt because it allows it to "put" all Islamic movements into the same category, which makes it possible to ban those movements on legitimate grounds. In this process the role of Islam is crucial because it is the common factor in all of these movements. Even though the Brotherhood would not articulate its goals in the form of violence (for instance, something like "Islam gives right to use violence"), it is being done by the government. This is one of the reasons why political opportunities are increasingly limited.

If the government sees all the movements alike, is it then possible that different Islamic groups would form a united opposition against the Egyptian government? Here the diversity of Islamic movements becomes clear. Even though an outside actor – here, the Egyptian government – would define all movements under the same banner, it does not necessarily mean that the movements could form a unified policy because their goals and methods are still quite different.

Violence represents a way to power for militant groups. The Brotherhood emphasizes the importance of working through existing channels and political structures but the militant groups do not see these kind of methods as meaningful. Thus, they see the changing of the political system as a rapid and revolutionary process. This is totally opposite to the Brotherhood's view, according to which change is gradual and relies on existing structures. According to Ibrahim Karawan, the militants challenge the government and also those Islamic groups who accept reform through peaceful means (Karawan 1997, 19).

The identification of militant Muslims, and associating them to other movements, occurs in a violence–non-violence axis. Here the attitude to violence is a more powerful factor in shaping identity than Islam. It has colored the relationship between the government and Islamists throughout the 1990s. In defining the identity of the Brotherhood, the government of Egypt has taken a central role: because of its policy the Brotherhood was forced to take a stand on violence and terrorism, and consequently on militant groups.

The depoliticization of Islam: al-Wasat

The 1980s brought with it more freedom and growth for Islamic politics. The rising tension in society led to the rise of violent and to some extent revolutionary groups which were suppressed by the Egyptian state, sometimes with rough measures. This meant, however, that neither moderate Islamic politics nor militant Islamism gained a strong foothold in Egyptian politics. If Islamic politics was a politically meaningful option in the 1980s, the situation had totally changed by the following decade.

Even though the possibilities for Islamic politics were minimal, Islamic discourse remained in politics and society in general. The impossibility of channeling Islamic ideology into the political system meant, nevertheless, that new methods of the articulation of Islam had to be found; ways that would make it possible to participate in Egyptian society without the state trying to prevent it by referring to Islam. This meant, among other things, a conscious effort to depoliticize Islam. One example of this was the founding of al-Wasat.

Al-Wasat began in 1996 when a group of young Egyptian Islamists formed a new Islamic party. Many of those founding members had been members of the Muslim Brotherhood but they had grown frustrated with the movement's work and status in Egyptian political life (interview with Madi and Habib, 3 March 1997). The registration of the movement as a party led to obvious problems, and since then the situation has remained unclear.

The goal of the group was to build its ideology on a base that would be approved by the state. Al-Wasat saw that the work of the Brotherhood had drifted to the point where it was not possible for it to continue under prevailing circumstances. One of the causes for this was the Islamic tendency in the Brotherhood's politics, without forgetting other methods of the Brotherhood which had been under criticism. The state authorities were not prone to release the ban on the movement. In spring 1996, the leader of the movement, Abu'lla Madi Abu'lla, was arrested with 12 other members of the Muslim Brotherhood. Madi was accused of endangering internal security and activating the work of the Muslim Brotherhood through al-Wasat (al-Gawhary 1996, 30).

As the name al-Wasat ("Centre") indicates, the movement wants to be a middle-of-the-road actor that does not favor the East or the West, neither capitalism nor communism. It seeks rather to build co-operation with the West and, at the same time, oppose the non-Islamic aspects of Egyptian society. In short, the movement defines itself as a civil party with an Islamic identity. In its program, the party says it will pursue democratic values and at the same time build co-operation (also) with non-Islamic groups, such as the Christian Copts and Nasserists (al-Gawhary 1996, 30 and Zubaida 1996, 155).

The interesting point with the Islamic dimension of al-Wasat is that the movement defines, according to its ideologist Rafiq Habib, its identity as religious and cultural (al-Gawhary 1996, 30). The movement wants to make policy where Islam is not political or a factor in defining political existence – that is, political goals are not articulated through religion, and Islam is not used in defining friends and enemies. Because the society is currently seen as Islamic, there is no need to move in that direction (interview with Madi and Habib, 3 March 1997). When a society is already Islamic, the people are Muslims in their identity, and thus identifying one's own group in relation to others through Islam is not meaningful, at least not in the same way as in pursuing an Islamic state.

Even though the Islamic dimension of the Muslim Brotherhood is not in itself an obvious or non-contradictory thing, there is still a clear difference with al-Wasat. For the Brotherhood, Islam is especially important at the symbolic level of politics where Islam is politicized. Political actors are distinguished from one another through Islam even if this does not give a blueprint of a concrete political system. Al-Wasat, however, takes a rather neutral attitude towards Islam and the group does not want to use religion as a separating factor towards other actors.

As a whole, I would call al-Wasat's attitude to Islam as culturalizing religion, which also mean depoliticizing it; thus religion is consciously transferred outside of political practice. This can be described with the term "*laïcité*", which means separating religion and state. Religion, thus, cannot be brought under state activities. This concept should be distinguished from the term "secularization", which means the decreasing of the importance of religion at a more general level.

In comparing the forming of identities of al-Wasat and the Brotherhood, one can suggest that the Brotherhood is more prepared to politicize Islam in its own work than al-Wasat. This applies to the Labor Party, as well. Out of these three, al-Wasat is less inclined to politicize Islam, and the Brotherhood is somewhere between these two extremes.

The Islamic community and state

In comparing the Brotherhood with other groups that articulate Islam in their activities, one can also notice how heterogeneous these groups are. Politicizing Islam and the political articulation of Islam has a different function for each group. The Labor Party has been prepared to politicize Islam even though its ideological background has traditionally been closer to the idea of socialism. However, it is not so attached to Islam in its ideology as the Brotherhood, which has made it somewhat easier for the Labor Party to participate in Egyptian political life. For militant groups, the violent articulation of Islam is one way of politicizing Islam. Al-Wasat, however, wants to depoliticize Islam and keep it as a cultural and private affair.

I will call the Islamic identity of the Brotherhood a "protest identity". The political goal of the Brotherhood's work is to present an alternative model for political action based on the present political situation. Identifying with Islam is the basis of the self-understanding of the Brotherhood through which differences to other actors are articulated. Belonging to the community and identifying with Islam is best understood through the opportunities for political participation.

The Islamic identity of the Brotherhood is, in many ways, linked to other movements, but in the end the role of the state is more crucial in forming that identity. When we examine the Brotherhood's identity it is easy to see that it appears to be quite different from the point of view of the state than that of the movement itself. The state seeks to perceive all Islamic movements as similar, and therefore their identities are homogenized. The state's conception is at least partially justified because every group unquestionably articulates Islam in one way or another – that is, Islam is present in every groups' ideology. On the other hand, these groups try consciously or unconsciously to distinguish themselves from others.

The Islamic movements form a heterogeneous whole where the political articulations of Islam produce a certain kind of political space. It must be noted, nevertheless, that if the meaningful political space for the articulation of Islam is examined in a wider perspective, one must go beyond the reciprocal articulation of those groups. For "Islam", the state's role in defining meaningful political space is crucial because in the end it is the state that determines the articulation of Islam, of Islamic actors, and through it the Islamic identity of those actors.

Because the goal of the Brotherhood's political work is to influence state affairs and shape them, defining its existence in the present context is a key to forming identity and possibilities of action for the organization. The state governs, by its action, the political space in which the meaning of political Islam is defined. Moreover, the state can define the political agenda where there is no room for the political articulation of Islam. Islam is interpreted by the state as a private and sociocultural thing, and bringing it to the political sector means violating the "rules" of that political space.

The state cannot deny the meaning of Islam in itself because Islam has its undeniable role in Egyptian society. But by limiting the political space and de-articulating the relationship between the official state policy and Islam, the state can prevent the political articulation of Islam in this context. The interesting point is that the state does not have to enter into debate with Islamists about the interpretation of Islam or whose Islam is the "genuine" one (c.f. Sayyid 1994, 48, 63).

From the state's point of view there are no different or more acceptable forms of political articulation of Islam, and so the Brotherhood appears to be as similar a political troublemaker as, for example, the other militant groups. For the state, the homogenizing of Islamic groups through Islam gives an opportunity to disregard those elements of the Brotherhood's political program that are not connected to Islam in themselves (one example is the 15 principles mentioned earlier).

The Brotherhood and other Islamic movements have succeeded by their action in bringing Islam to the political agenda – that is, Islam is therefore politicized but the state can control the political space so that politicizing Islam means at the same time an opportunity to limit those groups outside the political sector. The question of controlling the political space is, of course, closely connected to power; by controlling the political space the state uses its power with regard to other potential political actors.

It must be noted, however, that the state cannot prevent the *struggle* for political space. The Brotherhood and other Islamic movements strive to be the determiners of the political space. This process reinforces their identity, and in this case particularly Islamic identity. Political action culminates around Islam, and thus it will be articulated especially strongly in this process. Therefore, in the relationship between the state and Islamic movements, the demands of the political sector rather than religious demands will not be articulated, and therefore the central political questions (for example, freedom of assembly and freedom of expression) remain in the shadows.

NOTES

1 The Arabic name for the movement is al-Ikhwan al-Muslimum – Ikhwan in short. This book also uses *the Muslim Brotherhood* and *the Brotherhood*.
2 For the history of the movement, see e.g. Mitchell (1969), Carré (1983), Bari (1995) and Lia (1998).
3 In the 1984 elections the Brotherhood was in coalition with a secular New Wafd party. This electoral alliance received 59 seats in total (out of 448), of which the Brotherhood received 9. In the 1987 elections, the Brotherhood formed a so-called Islamic Alliance together with the Socialist Labor Party and the Liberal Party. Their slogan was: "Islam is the solution". The alliance received 60 seats, of which the Brotherhood received 36. More on election alliances in Singer (1993).
4 Interview with Kamal El-Helbawy, 18 December 1998. El-Helbawy has worked as a representative of the Brotherhood in London.
5 These demands are also partly expressed in other programs of the Brotherhood (e.g. *A brief note in shura* and *Our Testimony*).
6 Here I have used the English translation "The role of Muslim Women in an Islamic Society". There is another translation of the same paper called "Muslim Women in the Muslim Society".
7 These thoughts are based on interviews with the Brotherhood's spiritual leader Mahmud El-Hudaybi (Cairo, 22 February 1992 and 3 March 1997), and on an interview with Kamal El-Helbawy (London, 5 December 1997).
8 Other militant groups include Al-Jihad al-Islam al-Jihad (New Islamic Jihad), Al-Takfir wa al-hijra (Denunciation and Holy Flight) and Al-Najoun Min al-Nar (Survivors from Hell) (Sadiki 1995, 265).

3

The Internet: Myriad Voices and One Islam

Introduction

The end of the last century and the beginning of the present brought with them new structures that change social reality and practices. One of them is the Internet, which represents a social structure in which the mixing of local and global levels is typical. Also, the meanings of and relationship with time and place needs to be re-evaluated in analyzing the Internet. Furthermore, the Internet is creating forms of communality that are based on virtual contacts and experiences.

The Internet works through computers and networks, and people see it on their computer in a largely textual form. This means also that political "actions" – politicality – are expressed in this form. It is not a politics in which representatives can be elected to parliament or that would directly affect certain things. In this sense, the politicality of the Internet represents criticism against the traditional definition of politics, which was dealt with earlier in this book, and it is a clear indication of how politics has an aspectual nature. In the two previous cases, the space of politics was situated in relatively conventional political contexts. The case under examination here represents the aspectual nature of politics in its purest form.

The text that follows examines the political articulation of Islam and the construction of an Islamic identity on Internet discussion groups. How does the political dimension of Islam show in these discussions? What type of communality becomes possible for Muslims on the Internet? The central issues are the diversity of interpretations, the construction of an Islamic community, *umma*, on the Internet, and encountering "otherness". Primary sources are the discussions and discussion groups on the Internet that are connected to Islam.

Muslims on the Internet and research method

The Internet is a part of computer-mediated communication (CMC). This is a general title for all communication that occurs via different computers. In a technical sense, the Internet is a network of numerous information networks, i.e. "the network of the networks". The history of the Internet goes back to the 1950s and to the Defense Ministry of the United States of America, where a network called ARPANET (ARPA=Advanced Research Project Agency) was developed to serve the defense administration. It is regarded as a technical model for the Internet which was developed simultaneously in 1972 in the USA and in Great Britain. The development of the Internet went steadily ahead, particularly in universities and later also in the commercial sector.

The explosive growth of the Internet was sparked by the development of the World Wide Web, which came into use in the early 1990s. The growth has been exponential. The USA is the foremost user of the Internet at nearly all levels, with Europe next. Even though it is difficult to create a genuinely global system from the Internet, it is still quite global in a technical sense. The majority of countries worldwide are now connected to it, which means also that developing countries use the Internet more nowadays.

In Muslim countries, development has been different compared to the USA where after the original users, the defense administration and the academia, it reached commercial and private users. Interestingly with regards developing countries, Muslim countries included, there has been a stronger emphasis on commercial use than, for example, on academic use. Users have been quite elitist, although users inside university circles continue to expand and diversify the use of the Internet.

It is obvious that increase in availability and use of the Internet in a significant manner by various social classes has been pure utopia in many developing countries, at least at the moment. However, this chapter does not dwell on the usage or non-usage of the Internet, or its effect on developing countries. Here the text concentrates on those Muslims who participate in discussion groups whether they live in a Muslim country or elsewhere. The focus of interest is the inner logic of debate, not so much the external development of the Internet for the Muslim countries.

The number of Muslims connected to the Internet is hard to define precisely because the situation is constantly changing. One can estimate, however, that the majority of Muslim users are Muslim emigrants studying or working in a Western country. The greatest number of them live in the USA, but there are several Muslim Internet users also in Europe. Internet connections in Muslim countries are increasing steadily and the number of users will increase but it is hard to see that they will achieve Western levels.

One of the most important research areas on the Internet is discussion groups. The communication in those groups consists of public discussions, which have some features in common with the "letters to the editor" section in newspapers. As a communication form the Internet is quite unique. The existing ways of communication are present in discussion groups, but still it is a totally new level of communication. Discussion groups can, therefore, be regarded as "a global letters to the editor section". The Internet thus complements and gives alternatives to traditional media (c.f. Sachs 1995, 96).

Traditionally communication has been between sender and receiver, but with the Internet the situation is different: there is not such a great difference between a sender and receiver than before (see e.g. Morris and Ogan 1996). According to Pierre Lévy, Internet communication is "many-to-many" communication. This means that every participant on the Internet is potentially both the sender and the receiver. Normal mass media are of a "one-to-many" type where there is a clear division between the centralized sender and the passive group of receivers. Telephone is "one-to-one" communication that is based on reciprocity in the same way as the Internet. The difference, however, is that telephone conversations lack the global vision that occurs on the net as a whole, and does not enable the creation of a common context (Lévy 1997).

The logic of communication is different on the Internet than in other media where communication usually follows a sort of linear path. The discussions may bounce randomly, and may include elements that at first sight seem to be totally irrelevant. Discussions are not incoherent just in themselves but, moreover, they often form a netlike totality with other discussions and discussion groups.

For the purpose of this book, two kinds of online discussion groups have been analyzed. The focus is, first, on those that can be called "Islam discussion groups". They are groups for which discussion is directly about Islam or themes that are close to it (Muslim or Arab countries and their culture).[1] Second, are discussions of other kinds of online groups that primarily concentrate on different themes, although Islam is occasionally dealt with.[2]

The texts were found using the Dejanews program. The most important search was with the words "Islam" and "Muslim", including variations. The search was focused on one day, and the total number of articles found was well over 500. For the most important discussion groups the search was enlarged to cover approximately the previous half-year. Furthermore, certain key discussions were examined for a longer period. With this method, some 1,200 articles were collected, and after preliminary elimination about 200 remained for closer evaluation.

Selection and elimination of the source material was a multiphase process, and the first phase involved reading the messages. The search engine discovered all the possible messages where "Islam" or "Muslim" was mentioned, and thus some needed to be eliminated. Among eliminations were those messages that were incomprehensible, impossible to read because of some technical failure, entirely personal messages or those that had derivatives from the word "Islam", like "Islamabad". Furthermore, all commercial information, scientific articles, information notices, news and announcements were left out because of the desire to concentrate on unofficial communication between individuals.

First, the analysis tried to discover which broad themes come up, what kind of totality can be found, and how different debates might be thematically interconnected. The themes in these messages and discussions were of various kinds. Some of them were about private life, but there were also more general discussions that were broadly connected to society as a whole. Another broad division can be made according to participants: discussions among Muslims and between Muslims and non-Muslims. The themes in individual discussions were, for example, the interpretation of Islam, the woman's role, and the relationship between Islam and the West. One should note that in nearly all of the cases the language was English, and in some cases French, Danish, Swedish and Dutch.

Second, the analysis focused on how the material is related to the observations made in the earlier theoretical part of this book. Thus, the reading of the texts concentrated on potential politicization of Islam and its different forms in the context of the Internet. Specifically, interest was on what kind of conflicts and conflictual situations could be found from the themes that were linked to Islam, and how these conflicts became articulated.

Even though in most of the messages the writers' names were mentioned, the messages in the news groups were basically anonymous because one can never be totally convinced of the writer's name, and it cannot be verified unambiguously. That is why one can never be sure whether or not the writer presenting him or herself as a Muslim really is what he or she claims to be. This fact, however, does not change the analysis because when a message appears in the news group it "detaches itself" from the writer and takes its own identity and meaning inside the news group. In the interpretation of this book, the basic assumption is that those who present themselves as Muslims really are Muslims, and if someone is not, it does not change the logic of my inquiry.

As in previous sections of this book, the theme is defined in the earlier theoretical part. Here the interest is not in "finding" Islam in the discussions of the discussion group, as was the case in the Euro-Mediterranean Co-operation case study, where Islam was not explicitly expressed but had to be "discovered" from documents and the discourse connected to the process. In the discussions chosen for this case study, Islam is present as a presupposition.

Controversy and interpretation: the articulation of inner conflictuality

The arena of Internet discussion groups is a most rewarding place for studying politicization. Activity on the Internet and in discussion groups means participating in the discussions by producing texts. The conflictual articulation of conflicts occurs, therefore, in a strictly defined environment.

It is easy to discover the existence of conflictual relationships in the discussions. The important point is that those relationships are both between Muslims and non-Muslims and among Muslims. The conflicts between Muslims and non-Muslims are predictable, and through them one can reflect on and evaluate many familiar situations in a new context. The Internet brings its own nuances to the articulations of conflicts among Muslims because discussion groups form a suitable arena for conflict potentials which otherwise would not perhaps come out so clearly and directly.

In what way do the conflicts among Muslims appear? What is the totality of practices through which such conflicts can be discerned? Generally speaking, in the politicization of Islam there is a situation where someone's own Islam is defined in relation to another's Islam. The relation is principally constructed around the *interpretation* of Islam.

This interpretation is an essential part of the totality where the inner power and political relations of Islam are defined. It is a question of the politicization of Islam where the actors are Muslims and therefore the politicization occurs inside Islam. This situation is quite typical in Islam, but the Internet gives it unique characteristics that have importance for Islam in a broader sense.

The interpretation aspect has also been present in the other two case studies we've looked at but on the Internet the political nature of interpretation is most obvious. In the two previous cases, the articulation of conflicts among Muslims has occurred in a more "concealed" way. On the Internet, the communication between Muslims is more equal, and the arena of communication is more coherent. Because of this, the source material is also more coherent than in the two previous analyses.

The seizure of interpretation

Through the interpretation the actor, here the Muslim who participates in a discussion, can define his or her own concept of Islam. This interpretation is normative because other interpretations can be blocked by it, and thus demonstrate and define the uniqueness of a person's own perception. Through this interpretation, own and "genuine" Islam are constructed and the truth about Islam controlled. Discussions on Internet discussion groups show the diverse variety of possibilities on which the interpretation of Islam can lean, and on the basis of which can be produced an acceptable interpretation of some theme.

The first feature of interpretation is the subjectification of Islam. By this is meant a situation where Islam is seen as an actor-like phenomenon that has the possibility to do various things. Thus, Islam acts as a sovereign subject that speaks in its own terms: "Islam does not oppose women working [...] Islam puts financial responsibility for children and wife on the husband."

Through subjectification one can talk with the whole authority of Islam. The writer does not, therefore, take the visible role of interpreter but lets Islam speak for itself. The writer is a mediator of "truth". Everyone knows the "truth", but the writer tries to be the guardian of it. The writer does not place him or herself in a conflictual position towards others, as if we are dealing here with a question of problems and conflicts between human beings. Conflicts are dispelled by appealing to Islam as a whole or to those subjects (for example, God or the Prophet Mohammed) whose importance in Islam cannot in principle be contested.

The second aspect of interpretation is the producing of we-consciousness with the help of which own conceptions are transformed into a collective thing. This we-consciousness helps to unify all Muslims to one group that has a common will and perception of things. The writer leans on the idea of a unified Islamic community but expresses his or her own views through the interpretation: "We Muslims don't read the Quran to take a history lesson."

There is an assumption here that fellow Muslims are able to understand the meaning of Islam even if they are not specified. The text is convincing because Islam as a whole or all Muslims are behind the writer's opinions. It is difficult for the opposite side to use the same reasoning in its argument: there is no room for articulation because interpretation is final in principle. Opinions can be rejected, but they are difficult to argue against.

The third aspect in interpreting Islam in discussion groups is appealing to the sources of Islamic law, which is a typical way of justifying one's opinions. The following examples are a subtler way of controlling the interpretation of Islam than the previous ones, but they roughly follow the same logic.

> The *hadith* states that there will be an eclipse on the first of the
> month of Ramadhan and a lunar eclipse in the middle of it.

Got it. By the way, this *hadith* is not considered strong.[3]

* * *

Because he does not recognize the original teachings of the Prophets, and they are quite clear – see Isaiah 40, etc. – he does not recognize that same teaching when it appears in the Quran.

* * *

> Why, in Islam, is more than one wife allowed? Why?

Why not? What is not forbidden is allowed. Fiqh 1A.

* * *

Would you perhaps elaborate? First of all this says nothing about head covering nor shirt; What you are adding does not come from the Quran. Would you mind telling us the authorative source?

* * *

> Fouad, stop acting ignorant. Majid (m a m) asked you to give
> evidence for the blameworthly *tawassul* that you and your teachers
> are calling for. Majid (m a m) has no objection to the type of
> *tawassul* that was practiced by the Sahaba – which is supported by
> authentic reports.

I have looked through what brother Fouad has written, and can honestly say that his opinion is correct. I think that u are not just ignorant, but stubborn in accepting the truth, as will be shown below.

Typical for this type of comment is that the themes of discussion and problems are of many different kinds, and reactions to them are equally as diverse. Interpretations can be given even with vague grounds: often it is enough to refer to some authority on Islamic law. Interpretations can be justified by one authorized way, after which the possible other interpretations or one-sidedness of reasoning are ignored. The Islamic law often appears to be a timeless construction that does not change according to context. In the examples above, the writer's own role is more obvious than in the subjectification of Islam. There is a certain space for the articulation of conflicts and personal opinions.

The problem of timeless interpretations also holds true in those cases that try to emphasize the contextual nature of interpretation. In these cases, too, the arguments are mainly based on the Quran and *hadith*s. This interpretation goes one step further and is also based on rather unchanging doctrinal construction:

Remember, the Quran says do not take a verse out of context. This is why you should be cautious. A good-meaning Muslim may give you advice based on one verse; but that might not be all that Allah has said. Hence, it is very important to know your Quran – Allah holds each one of us responsible to learn (it is not enough that we ask someone).

The conflicts of interpretation culminate on the question of what is real Islam and who are genuine Muslims. This means that some forms of

Islam are not approved as genuine. This is reasoned, for instance, by appealing to the sources mentioned earlier, or it is given no justification at all:

> BEWARE of the AHMADI or Qadani cult, whose sole purpose is to trick people to join their "exclusive" little cult by pretending to be Muslims! They are no more Muslims than the Pope (except the Pope doesn't claim to be!). The *mirza* and his band have started a NEW religion but attempt to deceive people by claiming to be Muslims! THEY DO NOT REPRESENT ISLAM! Their religion is *AHMADIYYA!*.

The previous examples showing the diversity of interpretations were not so restricting as the kind of statement above that denies a whole group. It must be noted, however, that even if some group should be declared non-Islamic in some discussion, the logic of these discussions enables participants to "deny the denial". Thus, even strong disagreements can still be debated. This shows, for example, in the traditional differences between Shia and Sunni Muslims. Nevertheless, some see that Shia Islam is not Islam at all:

> To the Muslim Ummah, SIPAH-e-SAHABA-USA, Inc. (guardians of the SABAHA) urge all Believing Muslims to participate in this GREAT JIHAD, that Shi'a are not Muslims ...

And for some, the Shia school of thought means the only right form of Islam:

> Si'i Islam is the truth.

A declaration of being the only right Islam is an ultimate way of interpreting Islam. The interpreter draws a line between right and wrong Muslims, and also between right and wrong Islam. In the examples above, a difference was made between right and wrong interpretation. Despite that, nobody was said to be totally outside Islam; disagreement was about some specified thing.

How does political articulation show in these cases? The basic feature is naturally that this interpretation question touches and is directed without exception to fellow Muslims, not to other Internet users – for example, Christians. Discussion is then limited in practice, though basically anyone can participate in it. The discussion is understandable and justified only for those who have a right to talk about Islam – that is, Muslims who have at least some understanding of Islam.

The conflictual nature of interpretation comes from the actors' intentions to define the right attitude towards different things. Through interpretation the writer can lean on authorized Islam and define his or her own views. Thus the writer does not speak only as an individual person but also as an authorized interpreter of different sources of law. The conflictual situation is not between individuals, because the writers themselves represent Islam in general. Rather, the conflict is between different methods of interpretation and thus between different forms of Islam.

Articulation of past and present: the Islamization of practices

The methods of interpretation do not rise just from present times; a strong factor behind them is some kind of assumption of history, even if it cannot be explained more precisely. Interpretation and tradition form a close-knit and intertwined whole. Historical meanings are conveyed by traditions and go back to the origins of this phenomenon. Traditions are a part of continuity, where present and past is combined to make a whole.

The interpretations of Islamic law mentioned above are in direct contact with this process of mediating tradition. *Hadith*s and the deeds of the Prophet Mohammed are also an example to modern men. But as one can clearly see from the previous chapter, tradition and history are not just conveying the culture, they are also a part of political action (c.f. Eickelman and Piscatori 1996, 29) because through them differences to others are made, and authority is given to personal action. John Esposito says that Islam is an *orthopraxian* religion. By this he means that in Islam the right practices and action are more important than pure orthodoxy. Action defines what is right religion: religion without action is just empty (Esposito 1988, 68–69). The status of traditions in Islam is based on this primacy of action.

There has been wide discussion about the meaning of traditions in modern Islam. Traditions are an essential part of the action of Islamic movements and, for example, to the building of legitimacy. For instance, in Afghanistan the Taleban movement, which was in power from 1996 to 2001, had a distinct eagerness to uphold Islamic practices. Many of those new practices concern women and their everyday life. Women were supposed, for example, to wear the veil and were not allowed to work outside their own home. Even though men had to follow numerous new laws too, women could be regarded as the main target for the most visible practices.

The importance of women as mediators of traditions, and therefore as a sign for identity, is essential. This is also obvious outside of Islam, but particularly in Islam there are many demands on women which are viewed as fulfilling religious doctrines. These demands are based on the idea that these particular traditions are considered as "original" or "authentic", and thus they have the force of authenticity. In discussion groups, there are regular discussions on different traditions and the doctrines they are based on.[4]

Understanding of history takes a concrete shape through present practices. One must see, however, that in many cases there is no actual historical precedent behind this understanding. Hobsbawm and Ranger illustrate this with their idea of inventing tradition. It is a method of interpreting certain traditions as ancient, even if they are quite recent or (totally) invented. According to them, inventing traditions is most typical in situations where a rapid change of society is weakening or destroying old social models or producing new ones that are not compatible with the older ones (Hobsbawm and Ranger 1983).

In relation to Islam, inventing tradition means that there is not necessarily a particular doctrine by which some tradition could be consistently justified. In social processes some conventions become actual through politics and politicization. "Using" traditions or referring to them are significant in thinking the processes of politicizing Islam and forming identities. They are visible expressions of implementing religion or belonging to a group, which means building unity with other Muslims. For forming the identity, it is not so crucial whether traditions are authentic or invented because they are, nevertheless, believed in. In any case, traditions appear authentic to mediators of tradition.

Islamization of practices in discussion groups
Encountering the past and present in Islam, and the manifestation of historical continuity, can also occur in forms other than a distinct and typical tradition (for instance, women's veils and men's beards). Interesting cases are those for which meanings that have relevance to the continuity

of the community are attached to some totally ordinary thing or, in some cases, to an exceptional thing. One way of illustrating the relationship between history and the present is to take a "random" thing or practice for which one wants to express an Islamic dimension.

As an example of articulation of the past and present, let's take the discussion of having a pet dog. Owning a dog is not, of course, an Islamic habit but in one discussion on the Internet this matter was Islamized – that is, it was seen through religious references of Islam. Thus, one could say that the concrete matter, the attitude towards owning a dog, defined in its own part those Muslims' understanding of history and their part in it. The interpretation of Islam was thus connected to how religious understandings are related to this question.

The discussion started with a short question:

I'd like to know what the Islamic law is for owning dogs as pets.

The answer was just as brief and unambiguous:

It is forbidden to own dogs unless they are to protect your house/livestock.

This situation resembled greatly the argument in the previous case study about interpretation. The discussion widened and gained other dimensions. Evidence for and against having a dog was traced from different authorized interpretations, and the Quran and the deeds of the Prophet were used as a starting point:

I'm replying from university and do not have the Holy Quran with me but the Holy Quran does not, as far as I'm aware, say anything about ownership of dogs. However, in the books of *hadith* of what the Holy Prophet (peace be upon him) said, did or approved of, it is mentioned that the Holy Prophet (peace be upon him) instructed Muslims to keep dogs only as guard dogs and hunting dogs but not as pets. Dogs are not to be allowed inside the house as then the house will become unclean for prayers – this is because Islam regards dogs as dirty animals. Also, once a Muslim has touched a dog he or she must take a compulsory bath in order to pray or to read the Holy Quran.

In this quotation one can see how discernible habits of following Islam are created through an attitude towards a dog. If you are a good Muslim, you will, for example, undertake certain operations after you have touched a dog. The dog is not in this sense just an animal or a random thing but something in relation to which righteous faith and proper religious rituals are executed.

The quotation above emphasizes the meaning of the Prophet Mohammed as the setter of a historical precedent. The Prophet's actions are seen as normative. In order to be an authentic interpreter of tradition one must, in each period, compare things to the early days of Islam, and not so much to the developments after it. The possibility of historical development is therefore limited, even if it exists in practice. The present situation is not seen as a continuum but as a "remote station" of Islam's early days. The time of the Prophet represents the perfect Islam, and the time after it means distancing from that perfection.

There were also more intricate comments, in which other kinds of historical precedents were presented:

> I read the story about dog in Islam many many years ago but I forgot which book, I can't remember; anyway, the story sounds like this: Jibril a.s. promised to visit RosulALLAH P.b.u.h on a certain occasion, and He did not come. so when RosulALLAH P.b.u.h met Him another time He asked Jibril a.s. for a reason, and He said that Angels do not come to a place where there is a dog.

* * *

> Abu Yazid al-Bistami was not too haughty to learn from a lowly creature – in fact, he learned from the dog simplicity and humility, and to eschew haughtiness and fame. Avoiding haughtiness is a very fundamental Islamic lesson, since haughtiness is, in fact, what caused Satan to rebel against God (Quran 2:34). Those who are too haughty to learn from a lowly creature are most likely in fact those who need this lesson the most. [...] May Allah bless the Prophet, his family, and his companions, and those who follow his path as the blessed friend, Abu Yasid al-Bistami, and help us to be kind to all animals, and not to be too haughty to learn from Allah's blessed creation.

A historical perspective is also seen through narratives – not just through pure dogmatism. Narratives are a channel back to the early days of Islam, and a way to understand the world and life in those days. Through narratives one can more easily build a social context with which situations can analogically be transferred from past to present. The time of the Prophet (and the early days of Islam) are thus often a kind of "social database" from which one can find an example or solution to any problem.

Historical continuum and the Islamization of practices provide the possibility of perceiving one's place in the totality of Islam. Thus a person does not follow just the doctrine but he or she is part of the temporal totality of Islam and the practices created by Muslims before him or her. A Muslim living in the present can still be part of the Islamic community of the Prophet's time by Islamizing traditions and practices.

The following quotation approaches Hobsbawm and Ranger's idea of inventing tradition. The writer calls into question the interpretation based on historical knowledge and on the Quran and *hadith*s because, according to him, the concept "pet" was not even known at that time. Thus the question of owning a dog cannot be based on historical sources – even if many writers would like to prove that – because that question could not be presented in the early days of Islam:

> As nothing about dogs appears in the Quran, but only in *hadith*, my question would be: "What were dogs to those early Arabs?" Only when that is answered can the *hadith* be understood. I wonder if those Arabs – poor, malnourished, diseased – even had the concept of "dog as pet". I really, really doubt it. Rather, dogs for them, at that time, were most likely flea-bitten competition for scarce resources as well as disease-spreaders. Are the *hadith* about them REALLY about the same animals that live nextdoor to me or that live at my friends' houses?

In this example, the normativeness of history is denied – not totally, but only when it comes to owning a dog. History remains, therefore, an essential reference but its meaning is questioned and relativized. The problematic way of interpreting history and history's changing nature is touched, and thus understanding and interpreting things through history is potentially unclear. In spite of this, the historical situation is used as an example – that is, what dogs meant to the Arabs in the early days of Islam.

Islamizing practices means conveying the idea of origin. Origin can, generally, be connected, for example, to nation, ethnicity or – as in this case – religion. Through practices one can stay in touch with the birth of the religion and its first followers. In forming identity, the idea of origin is essential because it can be regarded as referring to a person's own existence (cf. e.g. Hall 1992b, 294). The idea of immutability is thus an important part of constructing identity. Traditions and different practices are the means by which the idea of origin is transferred to the present day as unchangable as possible. This way one can get an authentic experience of the mythical time that is taken as an undeniable example to modern men.

Islam's doctrinal and historical structure makes it possible to Islamize many kinds of practices. This also means that signifying and articulating new things through Islam – that is, Islamization – is possible in many different areas of life without it being considered an especially unfamiliar practice. Potential Islamization means that traditions are clearly political. Traditions and Islamized practices provide the ability to build structures and concepts to classify people.

The political dimension of traditions comes, therefore, from their ability to make differences towards others. At a practical level, these differences can be quite distinct because traditions – both "traditional" Islamic traditions and Islamized practices – are, in many cases, quite visible and recognizable to those who *don't* belong to that particular group as well as to those who do. Belonging to a group and the publicity of differences mean that this division cannot be ignored. "Carrying" tradition and presenting it are thus political acts in themselves because religion in each is articulated in a very concrete form which, in most contexts, is in some way a separating element in relation to the surrounding reality.

The question of authority is also linked to the political dimension of traditions. According to Muhammed Arkoun, tradition is a source of authority that gives room for spreading that authority. Authority is based on knowledge: "[I]t is necessary to know chronology, facts, historical persons." In this sense, traditions are linked to the interpretation of Islam: who is capable of knowing. Arkoun argues that wisdom is seen as a marginal phenomenon and reserved only for some (see Arkoun 1988, 63, 66–67). Because of this, knowledge and interpretation are exclusive by nature, on the pretext of which there may be limitations on who can take part in defining the practices of Islam.

In Islam the meaning of origin and traditions are apparent. The doctrinal structure of Islam shows already how the time of the Prophet and, in a lesser sense, the first centuries of Islam have been at the center of the religion. Even though from the point of view of constructivism that particular era is not religiously so clear-cut as we have been led to believe, for Muslims it is undeniably "the Golden Era".

Fragmented interpretation: "Various Islams"

In the previous two case studies we dealt with two closely interconnected practices that show the political dimension in Islam. The interpretation of Islam, how a religious doctrine is "transferred" to everyday practices, is a central factor in the politicality of Islam. Nevertheless, the concept of history defines action and existence in the present. There are two aspects through which articulation takes places – that is, a personal conception of religion is constructed and made known to others, and at the same time it is related to other people's views. As the earlier examples show, there is no unanimity in different Muslims' interpretations but they are very vulnerable to conflictual articulation.

What implications does political articulation inside Islam have for Islam in general? What kind of Islam is formed through these articulations?

The central notion is that in the discussions on the Internet there can be seen the fragmentation of the interpretations of Islam between different actors. The interpretation of Islamic law and the consequent governance of Islamic doctrine have always been connected to power structures: Islamic law affects concretely the possibilities of Muslims' life. Structures are, however, open to changes deriving from the social context because in Islam there is no similar centralized authority or organized religious hierarchy as, for example, in the Catholic Church.

The lack of a unified religious hierarchy means that different actors can practice the interpretation of law. Based on this idea, many non-religious actors have seized the right of interpretation. Examples of these are, among others, such political leaders as Libya's president Muammar Ghaddafi and Pakistan's former leader Zia Ul-Haq, who have actively interpreted Islamic doctrine (see e.g. Esposito 1988, 174–186). Additionally, the Taleban movement was an example of radical interpretation of Islam through which the organization aimed to establish an Islamic state.

Even if there is no strict hierarchy, the *status* of the interpreter has traditionally been important for the content and importance of the interpretation. In Sunni Islam the *ulama*, religious elite, can be regarded as *de facto* a religious authority in a historical sense. In a particular social context there is a difference between whether the interpretation of Islam is made by, for instance, someone belonging to the religious elite of the Islamic university of Al-Azhar in Cairo or someone from a local Islamic movement. On the Internet, social status has little or no meaning: in principle everyone has the ability to be an expert or interpreter of Islamic law. Therefore, it is not important who gives a particular interpretation. The important thing is how one can argue one's own views in the discussion.

Interpretation of Islamic law has fragmented during the history of Islam, and these discussions change further the systematics of interpretation. The drawback of this fragmentation and variety of interpretations is the way people attempt to monopolize control of interpretations and prohibit contrary viewpoints. Such efforts are rather futile on the Internet because no one is in such a position that final "judgements" could be made. Everyone is, by supposition, an equal participator in the discussion. The righteousness or value of interpretation on the Internet is not just based on who presents "objectively", or bases on authorities, the right interpretation.

On the Internet, the "truth" is particularly clearly a constructive thing, and therefore it is dependent on the concepts and values formed by participants in the discussion. The participants are thus to some degree independent in defining the "truth". On the Internet each actor gets an equal chance to form an interpretation. This is based on the fact that in discussion groups there is no prior selection of who can make interpretations. The reality on the Internet is constructed through participation.

The fragmentation or dispersal of interpretation means that control on the interpretation of Islam is diminished and the role of a religious elite is decreased (cf. Esposito 1988, 183), because laymen and less religiously educated people can also present themselves as experts and interpreters of Islamic law. Generally, those people are political actors whose motive is, for example, to legitimize their own policies by interpreting Islam, as the situation in Afghanistan shows.

The process of fragmented interpretation occurring on the Internet is one part of the development that can be said to have begun in the 19th century when Islamic modernism started to emerge. An essential part of this process of change has been challenging the interpretation of traditional Islamic law. According to modernists, *ulama* is a conservative organ incapable of interpreting Islamic law in the modern world. A part of freeing interpretation from old patterns was the idea that it is also allowed to others than *ulama* (see e.g. Esposito 1988, 130–136, 142–143).

The decreased control means that political articulation inside Islam is possible. The question of interpretation seems to suggest that Islam is a very closed entity. Through interpretation one can thus build a "tenable" entirety of Islam defined by the interpreter. This gives room for the exclusive and dogmatic totality of Islam. But this exclusivity and dogmatism is only a part of the Islam expressed on the Internet. There, no one can solely define the final "truth" of Islam; instead, different opinions are competing without any definitive solution being made.

If the interpretation were to be a closed one it would not provide the possibility of expressing contradictions, because in principle everyone would be right and agree with each other; someone would have made an interpretation that everyone would agree with. This kind of Islam would, in principle, be homogeneous and coherent. The Islam on the Internet is, however, heterogeneous. I will call this inner heterogeneousness "various Islams".

The interpretation means building self-understanding on the basis of Islamic doctrines. A picture of otherness is built through and among Islam's "own" forms. The "others" are other Muslims who potentially are also one of "us". Thus there is not just one possibility for the existence of Islam, but for each interpreter (or his or her followers) Islam appears to be different. Each interpreter therefore builds his or her own kind of universe. It must, though, be understood and reasonable according to the doctrines of Islam; it cannot be arbitrary.

Conflicts on the Internet are real, and they reinforce the diversity of Islam. It must be remembered, however, that the birth of "various Islams" is based on conflictual articulation. Inside Islam there is nevertheless an urge for consensus and for seeing Islam as a whole.

The Muslims in diaspora

The diversity of Islam is not restricted to the interpretations of Islam. It is also apparent when we examine the birth of Islamic communities in the discussion groups. These communities can be quite diverse inside Islam, if we use the same logic as in interpretation. However, the situation is different when we look outside of Islam and thus realize that the relations inside Islam are not the only ones that influence the picture.

The question is therefore: How do "various Islams" become one, and what are the possibilities and basis for building communality?

In the text that follows, the articulation of communal Islamic identity in Internet discussion groups is examined. The focus is on how relations between Muslims and non-Muslims are articulated in a conflictual way and in what way an Islamic community is constructed on the Internet.

Individual discussions related to interpretation were such that in principle they could have occurred in other contexts as well, even if they had some features characteristical of the Internet. When we start to examine the communality enabled by the Internet we can see that it is "place specific" – that is, the nature of Internet communities is different from other forms of communality.

In the case study on the Euro-Mediterranean Co-operation, I briefly touched on the idea of Islamic communality – especially how this communality is constructed internationally and particularly in co-operation between states. Here, I will examine the articulation of Islamic communal identity in Internet discussion groups. In the context of the Internet, the construction of Islamic identity is clearly different than in the contexts of the Euro-Mediterranean Co-operation and the Muslim Brotherhood, being much more loosely defined. This stems at least partly from the fact that the Internet is not a historically constructed political or social environment. The context of the Internet is an abstract whole and is freer from historical references. Thus the creation of meanings is, on the whole, relatively flexible.

Internet communication is special in the sense that those who participate in it surpass state borders and other political structures. The Internet case differs, therefore, from the Euro-Mediterranean Co-operation because in the latter context – even though it is international – the actors, the SEM countries, can be clearly reduced to a national level. Even though the nationality of a writer (whether the existing nationality or a former nationality) on the Internet has significance in some cases, it does not have generally equal importance with Islam.

The era of a modern nation state is sometimes called the era of "great narratives" for which social practices of a unified culture are typical. The present "official" political space is largely based on territoriality. The Internet and other technological innovations challenge the system that is based on nation states. On the Internet there is a new kind of global communality and political space, something where the social totality based on the nation state is dissolved and redefined. The Internet is thus changing our views of the world and construction of it (see e.g. Eriksson 1995, 49, Ogden 1994, 714–716 and Elkins 1997, 142).

Islam in a state of diaspora

The Muslims participating in Internet discussions are mainly immigrants or refugees. Therefore, the Internet is a means of communication for them, even though the communication channels to their former homeland may be problematic because of poor connections or the expense of using the Internet there. The discussion groups on the Internet offer a chance to communicate with other people of the same background. Muslim immigrants living abroad can find their fellow countrymen and religiously like-minded people through the Internet.

This situation can be described by the term "diaspora". In diaspora certain people or peoples live outside their homeland. This term is used especially when referring to Jews who are dispersed around the world. Nowadays this concept also covers any other group that is dislocated (see e.g. Mitchell 1997, 534). The Islamic diaspora, however, is different from the Jewish one. For Jews in diaspora their home is "the promised land", Israel. For Muslims, "the promised land" exists only at an imaginary level; it is not a state that actually exists somewhere.

Diaspora is therefore a situation *in-between*. It can also be called the *third space* (Mitchell 1997, 536). People in diaspora are away from their original homeland but they are not totally "naturalized" in their new environment. They are between those two places, in the third space. Diaspora is not then situated in a new environment but on a totally new level. With the idea of diaspora one can conceptualize the space on the Internet. There the space of diaspora is detached from a concrete space and re-formed in a virtual space. The diaspora on the Internet is unified *in principle*, contrary to diaspora in a general sense.

Communication through the Internet helps people to attach themselves to some unity and thus to be part of a virtual community. The community based on ethnicity that is formed on the Internet can, according to David Elkins, be called a virtual ethnic community (see Elkins 1997). The virtual communities formed around the Internet are geographically very dispersed but can be in contact with others through the Internet, and therefore the Internet is a suitable context for creating a diaspora identity.

The forming of a diaspora identity is influenced by the dominant culture – that is, the culture where people in diaspora live. However, the experience of diaspora means conscious or unconscious distancing from this dominant culture – not identification with it. At the same time, they approach the culture and the "starting point" that primarily defines the contents of diaspora. In this case the concept of an Islamic community is the basis for a diaspora community (cf. Tölölyan 1996, 29). Distancing oneself from the dominant culture means producing and articulating in one way or another one's own communality.

Articulation of the self–other relationship

The concept of diaspora contains an idea of togetherness and similitude. Togetherness is not in contradiction with the inner contradictions of Muslims. Unity is based on the religious grounds that can be agreed on. Unity is, however, created in relation to *other* communities. The inevitable and necessary existence of otherness for building identity is strongly present in Internet discussions. And the relation of self to otherness receives a distinct form. Especially, relations to the West, Christianity, Judaism and Israel came up in the discussions. Religions other than Judaism and Christianity are rarely mentioned. The construction of otherness (and self at the same time) happens expressly through the things that impinge most directly upon one, and the "West", Israel and associated themes represent these in relation to Islam and Muslims.

Western countries, Christianity and Christians

Relationships between Islam and Christianity, and also Muslims and Christians, have throughout history been interconnected, as has the relationship of Islam to the West and Western countries. These relations seldom have any concrete form, even though they exist at some level.

The Internet is an important forum because it offers a space for this encounter. Discussion groups offer a common social space where the meeting between Islam and the West or Muslims and non-Muslims can take place. The Internet enables communication that was not previously possible. Otherwise such encounters would hardly happen so naturally between different individuals.

On the Internet, the articulation between Muslims and non-Muslims is largely built around the same themes as those present in Western and Muslim countries' media, television and other public contexts. These themes are, among others, suppression of Muslims by Western countries and other matters arising from various historical events – each the basis for conflictual articulation. Muslims' status as the victims of the West and Christians is raised on several occasions. Victimization is a historically repetitive process for Muslims, and this state of affairs seems to continue according to these writers:

> I wonder what you thought about the genocide that went on in Bosnia?! They were after all Christians killing Muslims. Or were you as quiet about it as the World was!!! And you know something; many Christians HAILED the Serbians for getting rid of Muslims. And believe me, these weren't the ignorant ones either!!!

Being a victim means that communality is formed through negative experiences, in this case through suffering and death. If one member of the group suffers, then the suffering touches the whole group. And if some particular Islamic group suffers, then the suffering is directed at all Muslims. Collective feeling is strongly created through these kinds of victimizations: in the position of a victim you cannot be sure of your own safety and continuing existence.

There is no suffering without the producer of it. In this example, the Christians are, in the writer's opinion, to blame for the killings of Muslims. It should be realized, however, that in some situations the Christians see themselves in the position of a victim:

> Thousands of Christians are killed and enslaved in Sudan for no other reason than being Christians, and it is done by people who call themselves Muslims and the government is not taking any real action against this. That is the facts.

These kinds of discussions – even if they are separate – produce a situation of opposition where the relation of self–other is constructed on the guilt of others and on the innocence and suffering of self (regardless of whether these oppositions match with "the reality" or not). This opposition situation articulates by each blaming the other. This is thus a very charged situation because ultimately it is a question of survival and death.

Even though the relationship between Muslims and Christians is often seen as a conflictual one, this conflictual side is only one level in the articulation of the 'other'. As has been mentioned previously, articulation is not necessarily just political; it can also have a non-political nature. There can therefore be found in the discussions elements of constituting other that may be regarded as positive. In the following, Muslims' own views on their religion are compared to the views of Christians:

> Euphrates has assume that I "converted" to Islam. I did not. I "accepted" Islam. Why? Because I recognised the Quran as a message from Allah. At no point did I reject Jesus, AS, nor did I reject Christianity: I simply had never accepted Christian dogma, at least not totally. I never believed that Jesus, AS, was God.

An interesting point in these kinds of examples is that the relation to the Christians molds and reflects the Muslims' own conceptions of Islam. There are religious grounds for this relationship, and they are not just in the field of cultural policy, because Christianity and Judaism are, in spite of their differences, among the three "Peoples of the Book", besides Islam. These religions have much in common in both a doctrinal and historical sense. When Islam and Muslims are compared and contrasted with, for example, Christians, their own doctrinal grounds and self are then constructed.

This kind of comparison is often an unconscious action and it is not thus explicitly expressed. However, the relation to the West can be analyzed consciously. For example, the public image of Muslims in Western countries may create cause for concern:

> > I myself am deeply hurt that the first Muslim MP is being accused
> > of a sleaze allegation and I believe if convicted he provides the
> > example of a bad Muslim. Not all Muslims are that bad. I agree it
> > does seem weird that a lot of people of Pakistani origin seem to
> > be getting into trouble with the law, but there are some nice ones
> > around. I'm personally originally from Bangladesh and luckily
> > we don't get into that much trouble. [...]

> I think this is the real fear. Muslims already have a bad press in the UK. Most of it completely unjustified. We are looked on as a body as being anti-Western, fanatical and fundamentalist (whatever that means).

Here the issue is the question of honor and losing it, which is strengthened by the sense of shame for the actions of the Muslim parliamentarian.

Shame is collective, even if only one person is guilty of something. Shame is also associated with the implicit fear of estrangement (cf. Scheff 1994, 298); it is a fear of Muslims not being able to act correctly in a non-Muslim environment. One's own inferior qualities became articulated through shame. They are understood without the explicit existence of the other; implicitly otherness is present, of course.

The relationship between Muslims and Western people that is formed through honorableness and shame is not expressly articulated through contradictions. The example above shows, however, that this relationship is regarded as important and it cannot be ignored. This is an essential part of constructing otherness: the one that is taken as a stranger, "the other", is in any case a central figure in thinking the essence of oneself.

The context of the Internet differs from the contexts of both the Euro-Mediterranean and the Muslim Brotherhood in the sense that the relationship with the West is emphasized on the Internet in creating Islamic identity. This means that Islam is considered equal with the West, both in a negative and positive sense. In relation to those two other cases, the Internet is on a more abstract level, where the difference between actual action and the forming of identity is greater. The forms of separation are more drastic but also more complex because the political and social context gives more possibilities to it. The context does not thus limit the creation of difference and comparison.

Israel and Judaism

The role of Israel has been important in the political life of the Middle East since 1948 when the state of Israel was born. The co-existence of the Jewish state and Muslim states has been full of contradictions, and the question of Palestine has been particulary difficult. The question of Israel and Zionism would not have any general interest if it was just a local phenomenon. This issue is not restricted, however, to a geographical location but touches the relationship between Judaism and Islam on a more general level, and also Islam's relationship with the West.

Israel and Judaism represent the established, the "traditional" otherness of Islam. This situation has its own life; it is not connected to daily politics even though the situation is renewed because of them. Often the relationship between Muslims and Jews is linked to the actions and themes of power politics:

Now that Bosnia is rendered, now that 200,000 Bosnian Muslims have been slaughtered, Jews would like to replace Tudjman with a "liberal" President. In other words, they want to introduce a SECOND ECHELON into Croatia, and kick out the HDZ hard core establishment that proved to be a very useful tool for the killing of Muslims. Jews plan now to have HSLS (which was always in a stand-by mode, never going against Tudjman while he was doing what he was assigned to do: killing muslims) led by Gotovac or somebody like that.

* * *

If the Republic of Bosnia-Herzegovina could be saved, I would favor the removal of Tudjman, but, since that is obviously NOT the plan of the Jews, they only wish to introduce muddy waters of "liberalism" into Croatia.

Israel and the Jews are patently seen as an invisible force that has power to influence international decisions and crises. Israel is often connected with the USA, which is seen as an unwavering ally of Israel. Even though the USA represents the West par excellence, it is in this connection more of an enemy in power politics than in a cultural field. The USA is regarded as the guarantor of the existence of the state of Israel and its political status:

America has got the strings of the Zionist imperialist Israel … It is about time we united against Turkey, Israel and America, who hold the threat to peace in Middle East and world peace …

The relationship between Muslims and Jews is strongly hampered by the fact that the Jews have their own state but the Muslims do not, and this is concretely shown in the case of Palestine. The relation to the state is, nevertheless, different in these two religions. Israel is the promised land of the Jews, but the Islamic community is in principle not dependent on the state. Regardless of this, Palestine is an important issue for many Muslims:

Many of the Israelities never moved away from Canaan. As the years passed new religions came and went and many of them converted. When Muslims came the descendants of the Israelities converted again and became Muslims, and these people are present-day Palestinians. According to these facts the Palestinians can also hold the same claim as the Jews.

* * *

> I was wondering recently what would happen if devout Palestinian
> Muslims would pray to Allah to take revenge on the Israelis for
> them, instead of planning violence. Would Allah do terrible things
> to the Israelis?

It would be better to restart the Intifada.

The historical dimension is more clearly present in the conflictual articulation of the relationship between Muslims and Jews than in the articulation of the relationship between the West and Muslims – especially the holy places that have a symbolic meaning. The relationships between Muslims and Jews and Muslims and Christians are highlighted in the question of Jerusalem. It is a conflict-ridden question but is also something that unites religions:

> Jerusalem is a place that is revered by all the major religions of the world, and not only by Jewish people, i.e. Islam and Christianity.

Despite the differences, these three religions and their followers are, in many aspects, close to each other, sharing an affinity based on religious and historical grounds. This means that conflictual articulation is not an inevitable historical necessity because there is room for positive articulation, too. Here we see the paradox of constructing otherness: it cannot be an endlessly negative thing because the other is always part of oneself.

The Islamic community on the Internet: virtual umma
The relationships between Islam and Judaism and Islam and the West are not much different on the Internet than they are in other places, but through the Internet they are strongly and explicitly articulated. We can see from the virtual community formed on the Internet that the construction of identity is a multifaceted and situation-bound issue. Thus arises the question of whether one can talk of the birth of a community and, if so, in what circumstances. Are there any possibilities for constructing a community if there is no coherent base for it?

Through the Internet the diaspora Muslims living in different places can form a community that is unified in principle. There are, nevertheless, many inner differences expressed on the Internet and in the discussion groups, and therefore a community in diaspora is not an unchangeable or unified thing but a heterogeneous whole that continually transforms. The communities created on the Internet are most typically imagined communities because the whole Internet is based on non-physical encounters. The Internet community formed by Muslims is a virtual community mediated by computer. On the other hand, such a community is not artificial; it is tightly anchored to Islam's own tradition. Therefore, I suggest using a term "virtual *umma*" to describe the characteristics of this community. This term refers to the characteristics of the Internet and also to the Muslims' own concept of community, *umma*.

Identity positions connected to Islam and Western countries are constructed and kept alive during Internet discussions. On a personal level, the constructing of identity is obvious: in spite of a common heterogeneous basis an individual participant sees him or herself as part of a larger group – Muslims.

These Internet identities can be called postmodern identities, and they have different characteristics from, for example, traditional national identities. In the latter case, the existence of both individual and collective identities is more easily linked to common history, culture and geographical space. Even though identities on the Internet may be strong in relation to the whole system and to the community, it does not necessarily mean that this would also be the case on a personal level: the identity of a participator can be different in another discussion group. However, this does not prevent the identity of the participator being clearly articulated and strong in some discussions.

Communality is based on the possibilities in certain contexts, through which the carrier of the identity sees him or herself as part of an Islamic community: the community is constructed on these experiences. The community cannot be immutable as a whole or temporally because – as was emphasized earlier – the articulation of identity positions is a very heterogeneous process. It is interesting to see in the construction of an Islamic Internet community the complex nature of otherness, to which both conflictual and non-conflictual articulation of the self–other relationship is connected. This indicates that the construction of otherness and the constitution of self is not a black-and-white or clear-cut process. This means a more multifaceted view of the "traditional" picture of Islam versus the others, where Islam is seen as a whole that is having a clearly conflictual relationship with the "other".

The many-sided nature and inner heterogeneousness of a community means that there is no definite or stable Islam or Islamic community that would have a clear and fixed enemy or otherness. There are certain context-bound situations that can illustrate unity or timelessness, and thus these may be clearly articulated, too. But these kinds of situations are liable to change because of the nature of the Internet.

Virtual *umma* is a specific form of communality. This is particularly shown in the way Muslims utilize the structure of the Internet in building their community. As was indicated earlier in the text dealing with interpretation, there are more possibilities of interpretation on the Internet than in the "real world". Internet communities exist in a non-territorial form. They are not attached to actual spaces and situations but, in a sense, they exist in "nowhere" (Kuivakari 1995, 37–38 and Elkins 1997, 142). The construction of community occurs, therefore, in a dispersed way: time and place are chosen by the participant. Thus it is different from such social or political action that occurs in a certain time and space. There is no individual participant that could define the actual time and space of action, and their meaning for the whole process is unclear. Participation is not therefore dependent on a superior gatekeeper who would give rights to it.

Often, Muslims have been in a weaker position in defining their political space and respective political agendas and thus have had to adjust themselves, sometimes radically, to existing circumstances. This is connected to Muslims' lack of status as determiners of political realities, which has not provided much opportunity to create their own political space. The nature of the Internet is such that different actors can build their own space – that is, the reality mediated on the Internet quite independently by their own participation and actions. The idea of building one's "own" political and social space suits Islam's doctrines well. In a traditional sense, *umma* is by definition a social structure of all Muslims surpassing state borders. For Muslims, building a political space on the Internet means there is a possibility to exist as a Muslim and belong to an Islamic community.

NOTES

1 Most important of these are www.soc.religion.islam and www.alt.religion.islam.
2 Examples of these are, among others, www.soc.culture.pakistan; www.soc.culture.arabic; www.soc.culture.iranian and www.soc.culture.turkish.
3 The sign ">" at the beginning of lines indicates a message that has been sent earlier, and to which a message without this sign is an answer.
4 For instance, the veiling of women is discussed from time to time, and it is both defended and questioned in discussion groups: "Not wearing *hijab* does not automatically equate with promiscuity. I am a *hijab*-wearing Muslim woman, but I am still a modest-minded person; it has just never occurred to me that I ought to dress differently. The point being: we should not judge others so hastily, if at all."

PART III

4

The Concept and Strategies

Political Islam: is there one?

Throughout this book I have examined a phenomenon called "political Islam". At the beginning I mentioned that I would not follow any certain definition of political Islam. Rather, I have tried to approach this phenomenon with a more general question: "How is Islam expressed politically?" The theoretical tools I have used in this work have given me a chance to study "political Islam", or the conflictual articulation of Islam, from many different angles.

This examination has reinforced the preliminary idea that the politicization of Islam cannot be unilaterally located in certain actors or contexts. In each case, the politicization of Islam means different things and is made possible in different circumstances. It must be noted, however, that the political articulation of Islam is more evident in some cases than others. Individual cases can also change in relation to Islam: articulation can potentially strengthen or weaken.

If this phenomenon is so heterogeneous, can Islam be approached through a unified definition? It is certain, in any case, that there are many political things in the world in which Islam is present one way or another. The possibilities of definition are many and are particularly dependent on the starting points chosen by the researcher: political Islam cannot be engulfed objectively as a certain phenomenon of one's experiences.

Political Islam is, nevertheless, possible to define if at the same time the limitations of that definition are acknowledged in relation to the existing reality for different fields of science and their explanatory power. As a summary, I will form a definition of political Islam in which the central theoretical tools of this work are taken into consideration, especially the ideas of a constructivist position, the applied concept of politics and articulation. Therefore, on the basis of this work, I will propose the following definition for political Islam.

> Political Islam is a process where Islam is signified in a certain time and place so that the participants in the process are in a conflictual relationship with each other.

Essential in this definition is that political Islam is seen as a process, not as a quality attached to a certain actor, institution or doctrine. By this definition, the Muslim Brotherhood, for instance, is not unequivocally an expression of political Islam, although its connection to political Islam is created in those processes where that organization signifies itself in a conflictual way to other actors. The Euro-Mediterranean Co-operation, on the other hand, is not an Islamic context in a "traditional" sense, but it makes possible the political articulation of Islam, and that also holds true in the case of the Internet discussion groups.

Using this process-like interpretation of political Islam also means that the phenomenon in question is tied to conjunctures of time and place. Processes are dependent on the possibilities of a situation and context, which vary according to the time and place. For example, the capacity of the Muslim Brotherhood to politicize Islam has varied crucially throughout the 1980s and 1990s. On the other hand, the willingness of Muslim states in the Middle East to articulate their own interest through Islam occurs differently in the OIC than in the Barcelona process, even though the actors would, in part, be the same.

The idea of actorness is a central part of process-likeness. Political Islam is not, then, just an ideal space or ideological and philosophical way of looking at things. According to the definition above political Islam becomes concrete expressly through the actions of actors. Political Islam is connected to people and different collectives: actions produce political Islam.

Especially in the Internet discussion groups, the meaning of actorness and process-likeness comes out in an accentual way. On the Internet, political Islam is not present in the same way as in the cases of the Barcelona process or the Brotherhood, which are quite naturally attached to existing structures, ways of action and actors. The discussions on Internet discussion groups are characteristically an exceptional form of social life: they are "merely" communication between people. That said, participants produce, through communication, such meanings that allow Islam to be politicized. Without this process-like definition these discussions could not be examined as a dimension of political Islam because the political dimension of the Internet is clearly connected to actions, not to the inner qualities of a participator or structure.

The demand for the existence of a conflictual relationship is partly based on the concept of politics that was the basis of this book. Conflictuality is the basic element of the concept of politics used in this study, and that separates it from other disciplines. On the other hand, the conflictual aspect separates this definition from those definitions in political science in which the idea of politics is seen in a different way. The phenomenon of political Islam can be studied from the point of view of many disciplines and political science, but the idea of conflictuality defines in this case the "politics" of political Islam.

The aforementioned parts of the definition are general conditions for political action and do not, as such, have any connection to Islam. This connection is created particularly through signification. The idea of signification binds the definition to the contents of a phenomenon – in this case, to Islam. Linguistic articulations structure different practices and textual traces, and meanings are created on the basis of these articulations. As Mikko Lehtonen states, articulations "give a meaning its individual identity" (Lehtonen 1996, 217). Political dimension is created from the conflictual relationships between different actors which are produced by these meanings.

This kind of definition of political Islam gives a general basis for how the phenomenon of political Islam can be approached. It produces the minimum conditions for research that have also been followed in this book. The analysis is directed on *how* Islam is politicized – that is, the focus is on the process of politicization.

Finally, I will expand my horizon and examine the importance of these cases for political Islam generally. I will suggest, the basis of the case studies, three different strategies of political Islam. I have named those strategies as follows: the globalization of Islam, Islamism as a force of change and the emancipation of locality. These strategies are not the only possibilities but, for me, they are interesting starting points for further debate.

The globalization of Islam
The political dimension of the Euro-Mediterranean Co-operation, the Barcelona process, in relation to Islam is based on the fact that the actors are Muslim countries, and that there are themes in the process that can

be signified through Islam. At the beginning of the Barcelona process, Islam – as was shown earlier – had a minor role in the whole process. Even though it was there in the background at the meeting and was also articulated through culture and terrorism, Islam did not create any general form of discussion.

Thus, the early part of the Barcelona process continued in a relatively calm and consensus-like atmosphere. This did not mean, however, that the problems in that area would disappear or be resolved because of the process. One example of an unsolved hotbed of problems is the Middle East Peace Process, which has been one of the central issues in defining the international political situation in the Middle East both in the 1990s and the new millennium.

The peace process deals principally with the problems between Israel and the Palestinians and to some degree Israel and Syria. These problems are mainly local and deal with security questions. Even though they are not basically ethnic, religious or cultural problems, these factors have also been expressed during the different stages of the conflict, and there the role of Islam has been central (see e.g. Steinberg 1996, 90–91). Traditionally, the peace process has been a concrete showcase of the power politics of the USA, and Europe has had a minor role. At the beginning of the Barcelona process, the EU avoided deliberately taking the peace process to the agenda of the meeting. One exception was the prime minister of Holland, who emphasized the meaning of the peace process for regional stability (see Speech Minister van Mierlo voor de Barcelona-conferentie).

In the follow-up meeting at Malta in 1997, the situation was different: the peace process received far greater attention in the speeches of SEM countries than in Barcelona. They expressed a general anxiety over the failure of the peace process and its implications for the progress of the Barcelona process. For example, in a statement by the foreign minister of Syria, the success of the peace process was connected to the success of the Barcelona process; the latter requiring the former (Statement by Syria, 1997).

Taking the peace process to the agenda was also interesting from the point of view of the conflictual articulation of Islam. This meant that the relationship between Israel and the Arab states was being articulated through it. Thus, the whole net of problems with different actors and meanings was raised. For example, in the criticism by the foreign minister of Syria, the hazardous nature of Israel's actions for regional stability was discussed:

> It is to be regretted that the Israeli government has undermined the peace process in various ways, challenged the international will, the UN resolutions and the Madrid terms of reference, and rejected the Land for Peace Principle, backing away from undertakings and commitments which have been reached among the parties. The Israeli government continues, nowadays, its policy of building settlements and confiscating territories paying no heed whatsoever to European and international denunciation and to Arab anger, ignoring that this policy will lead to an increase of tension and extremism and the weakening of peaceful inclinations in the region (Statement by Syria, 1997).

The Palestinian opinions of Israel were most severe. The PLO strongly criticized in its statement the policies of Israel and its reluctance to follow the Oslo Agreement (signed in 1993 and affirming Palestinians' right to self-government in certain areas through the creation of the Palestinian Authority). In this connection the status of religions was emphasized:

> The Israeli government initiates a fierce settlement campaign to Judiaze Jerusalem and the whole West Bank and the settlement campaign reached its peak due to the Israeli decision to establish a new settlement at Jabal Abu Ghiem in Holy Jerusalem occupied in 1967, to separate Bethlehem from Jerusalem and replace Bethlehem with this settlement in the celebrations of the second Millennium of the birth of Christ. [...]
> [T]he importance of the Palestinian occupied Jerusalem appears as an international humanitarian and civilization metropolis for the interaction between the Tri-Divine Religions. The Israeli Government is now trying to Judaize it totally and wipe out its religious and cultural character. This needs immediate work to save Al-Quds Al-Sharif from the danger of Judaization, as it is a symbol of coexistence and tolerance between the followers of the Tri-Divine Religions and to secure its spiritual, historical and civilization status as a junction to the Tri-Divine Religions. (Statement by PLO, 1997; see also Statement by Egypt, 1997)

The peace process is not just connected to Muslims – mainly to Palestinians – as a people, but one central factor for Islam is the status of Jerusalem. It is one of the holy cities of Muslims, and keeping it partly

Islamic is regarded as important. Jerusalem is, on the one hand, the holy city of three monotheistic religions, but, on the other, it is a potential center for conflict where Islamic, Jewish and Christian worlds meet.

The importance of the peace process for the whole area cannot be over-emphasized. If it does not progress, then the problems involved may spread outside these countries which are now actually part of the conflict. The repercussions of this inflamed situation are likely to increase tension between Israel and Arab countries. Even though the contradictions between Israel and Palestine are mostly pragmatic, the situation can easily build to a larger conflict, with relationships between Jews and Muslims becoming even more of a bone of contention.

The politicization of the peace process means that the Barcelona process will increasingly move to an ideological level where symbolic and cultural meanings are taken up. In this context religions play a separating factor between different countries. Political differences are articulated through religion, because they cannot or will not be articulated through traditional political and trade issues. The peace process in these examples does not mean just areas of land, and it is not simply a legal or international political question. Rather, it is something that involves cultural and historical aspects, and the principal factor in making a difference is religion.

One central factor that represents a political dimension of Islam is involved in the politicization of the peace process: the integration of singular events and processes to a part of common Islamic consciousness. This means that Islam as a religious and social system enables collective reactions that rise from local events. Thus, the effects of the peace process spread outside the actual actors and regional borders. Islam is a symbolic reference to those Muslims who also take the peace process into account in those connections to which it does not "directly" belong.

An equivalent example is the Rushdie affair, which began in September 1988 when the author Salman Rushdie's book *The Satanic Verses* was published. It raised protests both from official political actors and ordinary Muslims. The amount of protest against Rushdie's book gradually increased, and in 1989 the criticism started to touch the author, too. The turning point was a *fatwa*, pronounced by the spiritual leader of Iran, Ayatollah Khomeini, in which it was stated that the author had given up his faith and that the Islamic community should punish both him and the publisher of the book:

I inform the pious Muslims of the whole world that the author of the book *The Satanic Verses* which was compiled, printed and published against Islam, the Prophet, and the Quran, and publishers who are acquainted with its contents are condemned to death.

I call on every zealous Muslim to execute them immediately wherever they find them so that no one else will dare insult the holy values of the Muslims. Anyone killed on this path is, so God wills, a martyr (Khomeini according to Schulze, 1991, 174).

There has been a great deal of discussion about the legal and traditional justification of *fatwa*, but its ideological content is unequivocal: the *fatwa* was justified because Rushdie's actions required redemption. It is obvious, of course, that all Muslims did not accept the *fatwa* and there was no unanimity on it (Schulze 1991, 174–177). In spite of this, *fatwa* provided the possibility of a large number of Muslims and Muslim countries to react against the defilement of Islam by attacking the book, the writer and the publisher. During the course of time, Rushdie's case received more general importance as an arena of the conflict between Islam and the West, and Islam and Zionism (see e.g. Webman 1997, 117).

The peace process and the Rushdie affair are examples of how the religious and social system to Islam gives room for "taking advantage" of global consciousness. These cases diverge from the meanings attached to a certain locality; they are *globalized* – that is, they transform to things that unite different Muslims who are living in different countries or in different social and political contexts. Globalization in this respect can be seen as global political articulation of local events.

This globalization is, in my view, a response to the (local) threat of Islam. It's a reactive phenomenon, not so much a conscious expansive intention. The articulation of mutual intentions is generally difficult because the actors should find some common and legitimate forum for formulating goals. Therefore, it is likely that Muslims' mutual disagreements simply prevent finding common goals. The situations may nonetheless differ when Muslims react against a common threat, because then reactions can markedly vary in relation to other Muslims but still, in some way, be unified in relation to the existing threat.

Globalization is not an inevitable or necessary course of development that would influence everywhere and unite all Muslims. Rather, the peace process and Rushdie cases "contain" a symbolic and cultural capital that could have an influence on many issues. The history of Muslims consists of numerous events whose importance has been conveyed from generation to generation throughout the centuries and through which Islam as a symbolic system receives its form. I would suggest, thus, that cases like the peace process and the Rushdie affair create and at the same time are part of "the great narrative of Islam" and particularly of its modern version.

In this sense the logic of globalization and more versatile media connections combined with the Muslims' centuries-old history offer interesting perspectives to the study of political Islam. Globalization interconnects things and events, and thus the consciousness is structured through common experiences. However, different people and collectives signify these events in diverse ways: the Rushdie affair swiftly became a part of global consciousness and at the same time divided people through signification. This global logic means, therefore, that potentially even the smallest of events can become something that unifies or separates large groups of people.

Islamism as a force of change

Out of the three case studies outlined in this book, the case of the Muslim Brotherhood represents the most traditional form of political Islam. It represents such Islamism, in my view, where a political group wants to influence a political processes and Islam plays an important part in its ideology. In relation to the existing state politics, Islamic organizations strive to act as a force for change that would effect the contents of the whole political system.

Islamic movements are often considered as essentially revolutionary organizations that come to power through rapid – either violent or peaceful – change. This idea is generally linked to the revolutionary tradition of Islam, which in modern times has been expressly manifested in the Islamic revolution of Iran.

The importance of Iran's revolution for the Muslim world has been considerable on a symbolic level because in various connections it is considered to be an example for Islamic politics. In this regard its importance is similar to the peace process mentioned earlier. The 1979 revolution in Iran is regarded as the only revolution of modern times where the ruling ideology and goals were religiously defined. The revolution was preceded by an era of difficult social, political and economic problems when discontent towards the ruling Shah had strongly increased (Halliday 1996, 42–51).

Even though the social situation in Iran and many other Middle Eastern countries was somewhat similar, the model of Iranian revolution is not a probable option for other countries. In order to succeed, revolution requires many simultaneous favorable elements – for example, support of the people, machinery, a strong leader and a predominately suitable social climate. This was all possible in Iran but, for instance, in Egypt the situation would have been different.

Islamic organizations are often dispersed and their ideology is not the same. Revolution is a very particular force of change and requires the conjunction of many elements. Revolution such as the one in Iran has been an exceptional occurrence that is hard to generalize to other countries and which is not necessarily regarded as a suitable example among Islamic groups. A comparison to revolution is not a just way of evaluating the force of change of Islamism; it should rather be seen as an ideological trend of Muslim countries. Thus, the essential question is how Islamism can integrate to political systems. The text that follows looks at two possible options: state secularism and maintaining a national status quo.

With the concept of secularism I refer broadly to increased worldliness in society. This concept can be compared to *"laïcite"*, which means, in a more narrow sense, the separation of the state and religion (see Göle 1997, 48–49). With state secularism I refer to the state's intention to diminish the role of religion on a general level and keep it outside of the governmental processes. In the Mediterranean and Middle East, Turkey is a typical example of state secularism.

The political climate and national identity in Turkey are a mixture of various sources: it is said that Turkey looks simultaneously to the East and the West. Turkey is considered a country whose national identity has received strong influences from Europe, Asia and the Middle East (see e.g. Önis 1995, 48–49). This has meant strict division with regard to Islam. On the one hand, Islam has substantial importance in the constitution of national identity and cultural self-understanding. On the other, Turkey's geographical position has brought along apparent European influences, including a secularist policy.

That said, Turkish secularism has been both a state-led activity and the consequence of strong European influences in society. Turkish state secularism has meant a conscious separation of the state from Islam and religions generally. Secularist policy was most distinct in the era of President Kemal Atatürk. Atatürk wanted to create a secular state in which different religious symbols or religious practices were not allowed in public. At the same time, secular ideology was introduced through education and the mass media (see e.g. Göle 1997, 49). This development culminated in 1982 when the constitution defined Turkey as a secular state (Heper 1997, 33).

State secularism does not give cultural and legal grounds for Islamic activities. For Islam, state secularism means that religion is systematically kept outside the political system, and thus secularism is a way of preventing the legitimate participation of Muslims in political life. Islamism is a threat to the secular state because it brings Islam into the political sector and leads to an understanding that politics is open to religiously motivated actions.

Islamists challenge the secular state system, as has been the case in Turkey. However, they have managed to achieve at least a partial compromise between state secularism and Islamism. Essential to the success of the Welfare Party, which represented Islamism in the 1990s, is that it has been able, and wanted, to merge into the secular political system. According to Oliver Roy, this stems from the moderate policies of Turkish Islamists and also the simultaneous "Islamization" of Turkish society (Roy 1994, 78). In Turkey the Islamic forces were able to integrate into political activities without any specific concessions by the state (Roy 1994, 125).

State secularism means, thus, defining the sphere of politics in a way that renders religiously articulated activity illegitimate. Keeping the existing political situation unchanged is one part of this. I call this status quo politics, i.e. an immutable political space where the groups aiming for political change are unequivocally kept outside the political process and the old politics continued. Islamism could be seen as one of the most important forces of change that potentially threatens the status quo. The problematic relationship between Islamism and the status quo is particularly apparent in Tunisia.

After the transfer of power in Tunisia in 1987 the new president, Ben Ali, wanted to present himself as the man behind democratic reforms. The possibility for political participation was enlarged, parties were legalized and in 1989 multi-party elections were held in Tunisia. However, despite being the strongest opposition group Islamists were still not given the opportunity to found their own party (Perthes 1996, 254). They participated in the 1989 elections as free candidates without any Islamic banners. However, they were not able to gain any seats in parliament despite their high support.

The political "thaw" of the 1980s in Tunisia reminds us of the situation in Egypt. There also the tension between the government and Muslims increased at the beginning of the 1990s. The government had been largely able to suppress Islamism, and many activists were forced into exile, to London for example (see e.g. Dekmejian 1995, 203–205).

The 1990s have shown that the repressive politics of the state have so far been effective. The Islamic movement has not received legal status and is marginalized in political life. One of the strategies of marginalization was to portray the Islamic movement systematically as a dangerous enemy of the existing government, civil society, economic development and internal security. The state also aimed to make Islamic movements enemies in a cultural sense, not just in a political sense: Islamists were a threat particularly to the cultural identity of Tunisia (Krämer 1996, 218).

Islamists were made the otherness that threatens national existence. At the same time, when Islamists were being made the internal otherness of the state, Ben Ali started to emphasize, after coming into power, the Arab–Islamic identity of the state. This meant, for instance, an increased number of religious programs on television, appointing a minister of religious affairs and reviving a religious university (Roy 1994, 217).

According to Larbi Sadiki, President Ben Ali also aimed consciously to make Islam a threat on an international level. Sadiki says that Ben Ali created the term "*fundamentalists' internationale*" – that is, international fundamentalism that is presented as the same kind of enemy as the old communist threat. Other Arab states tried to unify actions against this threat by internationalizing Islamism (Sadiki 1995, 265). Connecting national Islamism to broader international circles means that Islamism is "made" more dangerous than it probably is. This way actions against Islamism can be better legitimized.

My interpretation is that Islamism is not a threat to security as such, but it is a threat to political continuity, to the status quo. Islamism is a significant political force and at the same time a risk to the existing government. This is why Islamism is made to look like a national security risk, not like a legitimate political actor. The situation in Tunisia has continued for some time and no visible change or sign of relief is in sight. In Egypt the Muslim Brotherhood and other Islamic movements have confronted the same policies for a relatively short time. But without sudden changes this tendency is likely to continue in Egypt, too.[1]

The politics of exclusion

The example of Tunisia shows most clearly how the status quo is being continued, even if it means restricting political rights. The important question is the development in political participation and democracy. The efforts of Islamic forces to participate in politics and generally the recognition of their political existence has been a test of how the political changes in the Arab states and liberalization development has moved forward (cf. Krämer 1996, 205). These efforts have now met with strong resistance. The examples above show that the possibilities of producing Islamic politics (particularly in the form of Islamism) are quite limited. Further, if something is possible in one country it is not necessarily possible in another.

The question of Islamic movements is not about how they might potentially come to power in certain countries or "what country is the next to fall into the hands of Islamism" (Karawan 1997, 9). This is to put too strong an emphasis on the actions of Islamic forces, which are anyway – as we have already seen – strictly supervised by the state. The question is not whether the political programs and ideologies of Islamists are applicable or not (cf. Roy 1994, ix) because only in a few cases have they been able to adapt to political processes. The evaluation of the political programs of Islamists is pure speculation until we can see how they work in the longer term as part of, for example, a multi-party system.

The focus should rather be on how political participation and democratic development have been limited in certain countries based on the "Islamic threat". On the basis of this threat political pluralism is reduced, and thus the activities of movements other than those that are specifically Islamic are also restricted. Therefore, it is not only a question of political participation of Islamic movements but also of all other political actors as well. In order to prevent the seizure of power by Islamic forces, which is seen as a route to undemocratic development, governments practice undemocratic policies themselves.

Ibrahim Karawan has presented two basic lines on how the political systems of the Middle East have reacted to Islamic movements. According to him, they are the principles of inclusion and exclusion. The first means a situation in which Islamists are being incorporated into a political process by "conditional participation", which is directed mainly by the state. The latter means a situation in which Islamic forces are denied – mainly by suppression – the possibility of influencing society (Karawan 1997, 10).

In the light of the above examples I would claim that the inclusion of Islamic forces into a political process has not taken place, even if the states' attitudes have varied from time to time. In Egypt the principle of inclusion was not a realistic option at the end of the 1990s. It was a possible option, at least in a limited sense, at the end of the 1980s and the beginning of the 1990s, but after that the situation changed crucially because governments adopted almost without exception the politics of exclusion in relation to Islamic forces.

As a whole, in evaluating the future and possibilities of political participation of the Brotherhood and other Islamic groups I would come to a similar – quite pessimistic – conclusion as Karawan. According to him:

> Arab politics is unlikely to witness a wave of "Islamization", just as the projected triumph of Arab nationalism in the 1950s and 1960s failed to materialize. [...] The Islamists themselves have failed to achieve most of their objectives. This record of limited success is the result not of intellectual failure, but of fragmentation, political over-extension, effective state responses and the poor performance of self-proclaimed Islamic regimes (Karawan 1997, 11).

The importance of Islamism as a force of change in the future does not depend so much on the movement's own actions and efforts as on general political development in Muslim countries. The central factor then is whether Islamic groups are taken into politics in the long term, or whether the politics of exclusion will continue. Directing research to the conditions of political activity would provide the possibility of evaluating the dynamism between Islamism and other social forces.

The emancipation of locality

Islamism is not, therefore, a very realizable form of political Islam because the organizations that represent it do not have the opportunity to seize political space or participate in political processes. On the Internet the possibilities for political action manifest themselves in other ways. Political Islam is connected to communication in online discussions and thus there is at least a partial separation from traditional social structures.

The text that follows looks at communication on the Internet in relation to activities outside of the Internet, asking whether those consequences that emerge in the world of experience outside of the Internet can change this world. Examining the relationship between global and local levels is also important. The focus is on how global communality affects local-level activities and, subsequently, how local meanings affect processes on a global level. As Kevin Robins (Robins 1995, 146) mentions, virtual communities do not appear in a different world, but they must be placed in those new cultural and political spaces which are part of a larger social change.

Marshall McLuhan (McLuhan 1989) talked as early as the 1960s about a global village. This concept illustrates how the world was capable of becoming one whole. Global action and global actors are also a part of this idea. For McLuhan, "global" indicates the essential level of action. His ideas have been criticized from many angles: at the moment it is difficult to see a situation in which the construction of an autonomous global village would be conceivable. Connecting a global system directly to global action simplifies the diversity between global and local levels.

What is the meaning of these discussions with regards local action? At the moment, there are no structures on the Internet through which political actions could be channeled in a traditional sense. But the question is somewhat different when we think about the secondary effects of the Internet. Simplistically one could say that it is possible to channel the actions on the Internet from a global to local level.

The following message from an Internet discussion group is connected to a civil servant from South Carolina who made a strong attack against Muslims and Islam in a text that was published in a local paper. The text generated a strong reaction in the discussion group. There were demands for action against that person and people defended their own religious conviction:

ALL AMERICANS SHOULD RISE UP AGAINST THIS BIGOT, TO DEFEND THEIR RELIGIOUS RIGHTS AND FREEDOMS. MINE IS POSTED BELOW.

Dear Senator Hollings,

With great sorrow and regret I received the bad news that was published in *The Post and Courier*, 17 May.

It's shameful and inexcusable that the South Carolina Board of Education official, Henry Jordan, who said "Screw the Buddhist and kill the Muslims", was also quoted as saying the religion of Islam is a "cult" that worships "Lucifer" (*The Post and Courier*, 17 May). What's more shameful is that a racist like Mr. Jordan is still in his sensitive educational position.

This intolerant behaviour and racism depicted in Henry Jordan's statements against fellow Muslim South Carolinians, and Americans in general, needs immediate investigation and action.

This message is a reaction to racist and intolerant behavior that the writer says Muslims encounter in the USA. Questions particularly arise about much-talked-of hate crimes where an attack on somebody is based on skin color, religion or other ethnic factors. The situation is similar to a previous discussion on victimization, but the difference here is that an attempt was made to act for the cause in that particular local context. In this case the reactions also gained a response from the authorities. To a similar message as above was a response from the office of the Governor of South Carolina, and that response was also sent to the discussion group:

> Thank you for your recent email expressing your concerns about the comments made by Dr. Henry Jordan at the State Board of Education meeting. I appreciate your taking the time to write.
>
> I, too, was dismayed by Mr. Jordan's reported comments. I do not believe these comments represent the views of South Carolinians, the majority of whom believe that mutual respect and individual dignity are the cornerstone of civilization.
>
> Dr. Jordan has recently apologized for these remarks, and he now seeks forgiveness from all South Carolinians. I think it is healthy and proper that South Carolinians accept Dr. Jordan's apology and move on.

Complaints against the civil servant created reactions or at least discussion in that sector of government, and the civil servant had to apologize for his comments. Through the Internet this question has reached a far larger number of Muslims than those who live in the city or area in question. When collective action is channeled into action, individual ventures receive much broader attention than just in a local context. In this regard, this example resembles the idea of globalizing Islam as mentioned earlier.

The second example relates to a Muslim who was fired from his job at the University of Pittsburgh, and without justified grounds according to him. In his opinion, it was a case of religious discrimination. He asked for support for his cause in his message:

> In 1992 I accepted Islam while working at the University of Pittsburgh. This is correlated with increasing amounts of malicious harrasment from my (secular-Jewish female – Shirley Haberman) supervisor. [...]
>
> In October of 1992 I was fired. [...] It also had a severely negative professional, financial and emotional effect upon my life that continues to this day. [...]
>
> I asked for help and support once before on ARI/SRI [Internet discussion groups] and got some, and am now asking for your support once again.
>
> My initial requests for help resulted in a letter of support from the American-Muslim Council, and a letter from a long-term member of Amnesty International (who looked at much of the material) who stated that my complaint had all the signs of legitimacy, as well as many letters, faxes from the readers, both Muslim and non-Muslim, of ARI/SRI.

The writer is a (converted) Muslim and according to him his problems were caused by a secular Jewish woman. The writer sees that the problem is his conversion to Islam, and he wants support from religious quarters, which are for example the American-Muslim Council and Islam discussion groups. There were responses – at the same time the writer continued to send his message repeatedly, and used also WWW pages to give background to the event and to follow how the situation developed – including this one:

> I find your treatment by your previous employers is outrageous and indicative of the discrimination still prevalent in the land of equal oppurtunities. It is perhaps also indicative of the Western societies'

apprehensive and thoroughly unfair treatment of Muslims. [...] Could we not as a virtual community at ARI raise our virtual voices and ensure the appropriate authorities become more alert to this situation, e.g. sending emails of support to those authorities urging them to take positive action? I for my bit will be happy to add my voice.

The writer of this message argues that discrimination is particularly a problem because it is against the principles of equality prevailing in the USA: it shows in his opinion the unjust treatment of Muslims occurring in Western societies. According to his reasoning, the events at the university illustrate firstly the actions of the United States, and secondly he generalizes it (conditionally) to other Western societies. The fired employee is a person living in American society but he is also a Muslim, and in order to help him other Muslims as a (virtual) community should act against the local authorities.

These examples show how the Internet could be used in activating action in some situations that occur outside the Internet. An interesting point is that even if these events have a strong local flavor, support is asked for from a context that is as large as possible and that goes way beyond the local context.

> I need some ideas for what a group of Muslims can do for *dawah* activities?
[...] I assume that you are refering to *dawah* among non-Muslims. In my view the best thing to do is on Sundays to go to the neighborhood churches and present a very carefully drafted speech structured to inform the Christian American audience concerning the basic Islamic beliefs, the communality and divergence. The objective would be to negate the negative stereotyping, and lift the general fog of ignorance. [...] Our goal should be to change American religious awareness to include Islam, from just a "Judeo-Christian" state of mind.

As in other examples there is a fluent movement here from one level of reality to another. The global community appears to be relatively unified. The sense of action is clear to participants: unified missions unite. Communality is not just connected to communicative action but also has a clear action-based and emancipatory aspect.

The effects of global and local could be thought of from the whole system's point of view. One can make similar conclusions about Islam discussions to those made by Hiram Sachs in studying a discussion forum called the Peacenet. He states that even if only a small number of people are registered in systems like Peacenet, their behavior is already opening up new kinds of ways to conceptualize this media. Even more important, according to him, is the possibility that individuals can join together on the Internet free from political realities and participate in the discussion in this new forum (Sachs 1995, 98).

This possibility of free discussion is also an important concept for Muslims. Participating in the discussions and following them provides the chance of emancipatory action in relation to the local-level political actors both in a diaspora situation and in Muslim countries. Thus, the networks of existing power structures receive new dimensions through the Internet.

Emphasizing the importance of local action in relation to the system level in the context of Islam is connected to the strength of Islam as an element producing identities and actions. The Islamic identity conveyed by the Internet can be compared to other Internet identities and communities. Other communities on the Internet are almost totally virtual – that is, they do not have any counterpart outside the Internet. Examples of these kinds of communities are, among others, certain MUD and IRC communities (see Rheingold 1995). However, many of those communities are quite young. They have emerged with the development of the system, and attaching to or identifying with them occurs largely through meanings created on the Internet. In the constitution of communities, non-historicalness is compensated by interaction in the situation (cf. Mosco 1996, 122).

The Internet brings new elements to Islam and partly restructures old ones. For Muslims the Internet provides the possibility for a global community that is also closely connected to local actors and action. The Internet is based on the activities of individuals acting on a local level, and participants are connected to the global level of the Internet through discussions. Global communality enables the birth of such consciousness that in its part helps to realize action on a local level. On the Internet Muslims can detach themselves from the sectoral political reality (the same holds true for other Internet users) and they can create a new kind of political space. This space is free from the structures and power relations of everyday politics.

Communal emancipation is realized through personal action, which takes a concrete form on a local level. The emancipatory actor in the context of the discussion groups is not a clearly defined group, as was the case for the Muslim Brotherhood, but is a fragmented collective that acts on an ad hoc basis and whose members are not, in principle, in contact with each other. This means that a global environment provides an impulse to local action but is disorganized and occurs in a very unpredictable way. In this sense it is a good example of decentralized politics, which is independent of state activities and state borders. Therefore, it is also an example of the kind of political action made possible by globalization.

All in all, the strategies presented here can be seen as being ways of participating in the battle for political space. This battle is connected to the issue of who has the power to determine the political questions in different contexts. These strategies represent the political articulation of Islam on a general level, and thus the political struggle does not influence individual articulations, but rather it is a question of seeing Islam as a general possibility for political action.

The globalization of Islam means a battle for the symbolically determined political space. The peace process and the Rushdie affair are reactions to the threat against Islam, but they are also a way to mobilize such a collective consciousness where the target is clear but its significations extend beyond the target. With the peace process and the Rushdie affair, different Muslim actors participate in defining the political space. It must be noted, however, that it is a dispersed process on the level of action – that is, in spite of common consciousness there is no unified way of action that would determine the process.

In relation to Islam, the battle for political space is localized, and therefore it is quite well known how the process works and who or what the significant actors are. The control of political space is connected to the justification of social existence, and thus to the participation of concrete political processes – for example, elections. On the basis of these examples, one could say that Islamists are incapable of participating in the control of existing political space, and, furthermore, they are unable to build their own political space for their demands.

The emancipation of locality is connected to local action but, contrary to the case of Islamism, the action through the Internet is dispersed in unpredictable ways to different geographical contexts. The control of political space is interaction between communication on a global level, on the Internet, and action at a local level. Political questions arise from the situations at a local level, and they return to a local level through action. Political space is, in this case, fragmented because local situations and problems are separate. They are, however, articulated in principle at a common global level by using the collective consciousness.

The political spaces that are articulated in an Islamic way express for their part the heterogeneousness of political Islam. In the end, one must remember that Islam in itself – and in its own heterogeneousness – represents unity in its multiplicity. Identification with Islam creates an impression of belonging together and to the same ideal Islamic community, even though every member and collective produces in their own unique way their own identity in relation to the existing totality of Islam.

NOTES

1 The development in Algeria since the beginning of the 1990s has meant returning to this status quo thinking. At the beginning of the decade Islamic forces were allowed to participate in the political processes, but after their election victory these organizations were declared illegal.

Bibliography

Literature

Al-Ahsan, ʿAbdullah (1988) *OIC: The Organization of Islamic Conference.* Herndon: The International Institute of Islamic Thought.

Al-Gawhary, Karim (1996) "We are a Civil Party with an Islamic Identity". An Interview with Abu ʿIla Madi Abu ʿIla and Rafiq Habib. *Middle East Report.* April–June.

Aliboni, Roberto (1996) *The Euro-Mediterranean Partnership: An Interpretation from Italy.* www.diplomacy.edu/conf/abarcel2/papers/aliboni.html; 12 November 1997.

Anderson, Benedict (1991) (1983) *Imagined Communities.* London & New York: Verso.

Arkoun, Muhammed (1988) "The Concept of Authority in Islamic Thought". In Klaus Ferdinand and Mehdi Mozaffari (eds) *Islam: State and Society.* Studies on Asian Topics, No. 12. London & Riverdale: Curzon Press & The Riverdale Company.

Arkoun, Muhammed (1994) (1989) *Rethinking Islam: Common Questions, Uncommon Answers.* Robert D. Lee (translated and edited). Boulder, San Francisco & Oxford: Westview Press.

Auda, Gehad (1991) "An Uncertain Response: The Islamic Movement in Egypt". In James Piscatori (ed.) *Islamic Fundamentalism and the Gulf Crisis.* The Fundamentalism Project. Chicago: American Academy of Art Sciences.

Ayalon, Ami (1997) "Egypt (Jumhuriyyat Misr al-ʾArabiyya)". In Bruce Maddy-Weitzman (ed.) *Middle East Contemporary Survey.* Vol. XIX: 1995. Boulder, San Francisco & Oxford: Westview Press.

Ayubi, Nazih (1991) *Political Islam, Religion and the Politics in the Arab World.* London: Routledge.

Ayubi, Nazih N. (1995) "Rethinking the Public/Private Dichotomy: Radical Islamism and Civil Society in the Middle East". *Contention.* Vol. 4, No. 3.

Badey, Thomas J. (1998) "Defining International Terrorism: A Pragmatic Approach". *Terrorism and Political Violence.* Vol. 10, No. 1.

Barakat, Halim (1993) *The Arab World. Society, Culture, and State.* Berkeley, Los Angeles & Oxford: University of California Press.

Bari, Zohurul (1995) *Re-emergence of the Muslim Brothers in Egypt.* New Delhi: Lancers Books.

Botiveau, Bernard (1993) "Contemporary Reinterpretations of Islamic Law: The Case of Egypt". In Chibli Mallat (ed.) *Islam and Public Law.* London: Graham & Trotman.

Bouchat, Clarence J. (1996) "A Fundamentalist Islamic Threat to the West". *Studies in Conflict & Terrorism.* Vol. 19, s. 339–352.

Butter, David (1994) "Hopes Pinned on Economic Revival". *MEED.* No. 22, 3 June.

Calleya, Stephen C. (1998) "Crosscultural Currents in the Mediterranean: What Prospects?" *Mediterranean Quarterly.* Vol. 9, No. 3.

Carré, O. G. Michaud (1983) "*Les frères musulmans 1928–1982*". Paris: Gallimard.

Cerny, Philip R. (1996) "Globalization and other Stories: The Search for a New Paradigm for International Relations". *International Journal.* Vol. LI, No. 4.

Dekmejian, R. Hrair (1995) *Islam in Revolution: Fundamentalism in the Arab World.* Syracuse & New York: Syracuse University Press.

Eickelman, Dale F. and Piscatori, James (1996) *Muslim Politics.* Princeton, New Jersey: Princeton University Press.

Elkins, David J. (1997) "Globalization, Telecommunication, and Virtual Ethnic Communities". *International Political Science Review.* Vol. 18, No. 2.

Eriksson, Kai (1995) "Internet ja moderni julkisuus". *Lähikuva.* No. 1.

Esposito, John (1983) "Introduction: Islam and Muslim Politics". In John Esposito (ed.) *Voices of Resurgent Islam.* New York & Oxford: Oxford University Press.

—(1987) *Islam and Politics.* New York: Syracuse University Press.

—(1988) *Islam: The Straight Path.* New York & Oxford: Oxford University Press.

European Commission (1997) *Euro-Mediterranean Partnership.* March.

Fandy, Mamoun (1993) "The Tensions Behind the Violence in Egypt". *Middle East Policy.* Vol. 2, No. 1.

Fenech, Dominic (1997) "The Relevance of European Security Structures to the Mediterranean (and Vice Versa)". *Mediterranean Politics.* Vol. 2, No. 1, Summer.

fòrum civil euromed (1996) *Towards a New Scenario of Partnership in the Euro-Mediterranean Area*. Barcelona: Institut Català de la Mediterrània.

Fuller, Graham E. and Lesser, Ian O. (1995) *A Sense of Siege: The Geopolitics of Islam and the West*. Boulder, San Francisco & Oxford: Westview Press.

Ginsberg, Roy Howard (1990) *Foreign Policy Actions of the European Community*. London: Lynne Rienner Publishers.

Goldstein, Jonah and Rayner, Jeremy (1994) "The Politics of Identity in the Late Modern Society". *Theory and Society*. Vol. 23, s. 367–384.

Goonatilake, Susantha (1991) "The Self Wandering Between Cultural Localization and Globalization". In Jan Nederveen Pieterse and Bhikhu Parekh (eds) *The Decolonization of Imagination, Culture, Knowledge and Power*. London & New Jersey: Zed Books Ltd.

Grimaud, Nicole (1996) "Tunisia: Between Control and Liberalization". *Mediterranean Politics*. Vol. 1, No. 1, Summer.

Grossberg, Lawrence (1995) "*Mielihyvän kytkennät*". Tampere: Vastapaino.

Göle, Nilüfer (1997) "Secularism and Islamism in Turkey: The Making of Elites and Counter-Elites". *Middle East Journal*. Vol. 51, No. 1, Winter.

Hall, Stuart (1992a) *Kulttuurin ja politiikan murroksia*. Jyväskylä: Vastapaino.

—(1992b) "The Question of Cultural Identity". In Stuart Hall, David Held and Tony McGrew (eds) *Modernity and its Futures*. Cambridge: Polity Press.

Halliday, Fred (1996) *Islam and the Myth of Confrontation. Religion and Politics in the Middle East*. London: I.B. Tauris.

Hassner, Pierre (1993) "Beyond Nationalism and Internationalism: Ethnicity and World Order". *Survival*. Vol. 35, No. 2, Summer.

Heper, Metin (1997) "Islam and Democracy in Turkey: Toward a Reconciliation?" *Middle East Journal*. Vol. 51, No. 1, Winter.

Hermassi, Abdelbaki (1993) "State, Legitimacy, and Democratization in the Maghreb". In Ellis Goldberg, Resat Kasaba and Joel Migdal (eds) *Rules and Rights in the Middle East: Democracy, Law, and Society*. Seattle & London: University of Washington Press.

Hobsbawm, Eric and Ranger, Terence (1983) *The Invention of Tradition*. Cambridge: Cambridge University Press.

Human Rights Watch, World Report (1997) New York, Washington, London, Brussels: Human Rights Watch.

Hunter, Shireen T. (1995) "New Global Trends in Culture and Identity". *The International Spectator*. Vol. XXX, No. 2, April–June.

Ismael, Tareq Y. and Ismael Jacquelines (1991) "Political Heritage of Islam". In Tareq Y. Ismael and Jacquelines Ismael (eds) *Politics and Government in the Middle East and North Africa*. Miami: Florida International University Press.

Joffé, George (1994) "The European Union and Maghreb". In Richard Gillespie (ed.) *Mediterranean Politics*. Vol. I. London: Pinter Publishers and Cranbury: Associated University Press.

—(1997) "Southern Attitudes towards an Integrated Mediterranean Region". *Mediterranean Politics*. Vol. 2, No. 1, Summer.

Jones, Steven G. (1995) "Understanding Community in the Information Age". In Steven G. Jones (ed.) *CyberSociety: Computer-Mediated Communication and Community*. Thousand Oaks, London & New Delhi: SAGE Publications.

Karawan, Ibrahim A. (1997) *The Islamist Impasse*. Adelphi Paper 314. New York: Oxford University Press.

Kepel, Gilles (1995) "Islamists versus the State in Egypt and Algeria". *Daedalus*. Vol. 124, No. 3, Summer.

Ketola, Kimmo (1997) "Mitä on uskontotiede?" In Kimmo Ketola, Simo Korkee, Heikki Pesonen, Ilkka Pyysiäinen, Tuula Sakaranaho and Tom Sjöblom *Näköaloja uskontoon. Uskontotieteen ajankohtaisia suuntauksia*. Helsinki: Yliopistopaino.

Khader, Bichara (1995) *Le Partenariat Euro-Méditerranéen*. Les Cahiers du Monde Arabe. No. 119–120. Louvain: Univérsite catholique de Louvain.

Kienle, Eberhard (1998) "Destabilization through Partnership? Euro-Mediterranean Relations after the Barcelona Declaration". *Mediterranean Politics*. Vol. 3, No. 2.

King, Russell and Donati, Marco (1999) "The 'Divided' Mediterranean: Re-defining European Relationships". In Ray Hudson and Allan M. Williams (eds) *Divided Europe: Society and Territory*. London & Thousands Oaks & New Delhi: Sage Publications.

Krämer, Gudrun (1996) (1994). "The Integration of Integrists". In Ghassan Salame (ed.) *Democracy without Democrats: The Renewal of Politics in the Muslim World*. London & New York: I.B. Tauris Publishers.

Kuivakari, Seppo (1995) "Sensoria. Postmoderni mediatajunta". *Lähikuva.* No. 1.

Laclau, Ernesto (1994) "Introduction". In Ernesto Laclau (ed.) *The Making of Political Identities.* London & New York: Verso.

Laclau, Ernesto and Mouffe, Chantal (1985) *Hegemony and Socialist Strategy: Towards a Radical Democratic Politics.* London: Verso.

Lehtonen, Heikki (1990) *Yhteisö.* Tampere: Vastapaino.

—(1996) *Merkitysten maailma.* Tampere: Vastapaino.

Lévy, Pierre (1997) *Collective Intelligence and its Objects: Many-to-Many Communication in a "Meaning World".* www.design-inst.nl/doors-doors3/transcripts/Levy.html#A; 22 October 1997.

Lia, Brynjar (1998) *The Society of the Muslim Brothers in Egypt: The Rise of an Islamic Mass Movement, 1928–1942.* Foreword by Jamal al-Banna. Reading: Ithaca Press.

Lorca, Alejandro and Nuñes, Jesus A. (1993) "EC–Maghrab Relations: A Global Policy for Centre–Periphery Interdependence". *The International Spectator.* Vol. XXVII, No. 3, July–September.

Makram-Ebeid, Mona (1989) "Political Opposition in Egypt: Democratic Myth or Reality?" *Middle East Journal.* Vol. 43, No. 3.

—(1996) "Egypt's 1995 Elections: One Step Forward, Two Steps Back?" *Middle East Policy.* Vol. IV, No. 3, March.

—(1997) *Barcelona and Prospects for Euro-Mediterranean Relations: Cultural and Social Dimensions.* Malta, 11–13 April 1997.

Marks, Jon (1996) "High Hopes and Low Motives: The New Euro-Mediterranean Partnership Initiative". *Mediterranean Politics.* Vol. 1, No. 1. Summer.

McLuhan, Marshall (1989) *The Global Village.* New York: Oxford University Press.

McNay, Lois (1992) *Foucault and Feminism.* Cambridge: Polity Press.

Meijer, Roel (1996) "The Problems of Integration: The State and Moderate Islamic Movements in Egypt, Jordan, and Palestine". *JIME Review.* Spring.

Melasuo, Tuomo (1991a) "Islam – sota, rauha ja politiikka". *YK-tiedote.* No. 1.

—(1991b) "Uskonto ja politiikka – islam kansainvälisissä suhteissa". *Ulkopolitiikka.* No. 2.

Mitchell, Katharyne (1997) "Different Diasporas and the Hype of Hybridity". *Society and Space.* Vol. 15, No. 5.

Mokros, Hartmut B. (1996) "From Information and Behaviour to Interaction and Identity". In Hartmut Mokros (ed.) *Interaction & Identity*. New Brunswick & London: Transaction Publishers.

Morris, Merrill and Ogan, Christine (1996) "The Internet as Mass Medium". *Journal of Communication*. Vol. 46, No. 1, Winter.

Mortimer, Edward (1994) "Europe and the Mediterranean: The Security Dimension". In Peter Ludlow (ed.) *Europe and the Mediterranean*. London & New York: Brassey.

Mosco, Vincent (1996) "Myths along the Information Highway". *Peace Review*. Vol. 8, No. 1.

Mubarak, Hisham (1997) "What does the Gama'a Islamiyya Want? Interview with Tal'at Fu'ad Qasim". In Joel Beinin and Joe Stork (eds) *Political Islam: Essays from Middle East Report*. Berkeley & Los Angeles: University of California Press.

Najjar, Fauzi M. (1992) "The Application of Sharia Laws in Egypt". *Middle East Policy*. Vol. 1, No. 3.

Neumann, Iver B. and Welsch, Jennifer M. (1991) "The Other in European Self-definition: An Addendum to the Literature on International Society". *Review of International Studies*. Vol. 17, No. 4.

Ogden, Michael R. (1994) "Politics in Parallel Universe: Is there a Future for Cyberdemocracy?" *Futures*. Vol. 26, No. 7.

Önis, Ziay (1995) "Turkey in the Post-Cold War Era: In Search of Identity". *Middle East Journal*. Vol. 49, No. 1, Winter.

Palonen, Kari (1979) *Mitä politiikka on? Luonnos politiikan tutkimuksen perusteiksi*. Jyväskylä: Jyväskylän yliopisto.

—(1988a) *Tekstistä politiikkaan. Johdatusta tulkintataitoon*. Tampere: Vastapaino.

—(1988b) "The Study of Politics as a Project and as an Institution". In Dag Anckar and Erkki Berndtson (eds) *Political Science between the Past and the Future*. Helsinki: The Finnish Political Science Association.

—(1993) *Politikointi – politisointi – politiikka. Tulkinta politiikan ajatusmuodon pelikieliaikatiloista*. Jyväskylä: Jyväskylän yliopisto, Valtio-opin laitos, opetusmonisteita.

—(1997) *Kootut retoriikat. Esimerkkejä politiikan luennasta*. SoPhi, Yhteiskuntatieteiden, valtio-opin ja filosofian julkaisuja 11. Jyväskylä: Jyväskylän yliopisto.

Pekonen, Kyösti (1993) "Nimet poliittisessa symboliikassa". In Heikki Nyyssönen (ed.) *Nimet poliittisessa retoriikassa*. Jyväskylän yliopisto: Valtio-opin laitos, Julkaisuja 66. Jyväskylä.

—(1995) "Puolueohjelman idea". In Eeva Aarnio and Jukka Kanerva (eds) *Puolueohjelmatutkimuksen nykysuunnat*. Jyväskylä: Jyväskylän yliopisto, Valtio-opin laitos.

Perthes, Volker (1996) (1994) "The Private Sector, Economic Liberalization, and the Prospects of Democratization: The Case of Syria and some other Arab Countries". In Ghassan Salame (ed.) *Democracy without Democrats: The Reneval of Politics in the Muslim World*. London & New York: I.B. Tauris Publishers.

Piscatori, James P. (1988) *Islam in the World of Nation-States*. Cambridge: The Press Syndicate of the University of Cambridge.

Räisänen, Heikki (1986) *Koraani ja Raamattu*. Helsinki: Gaudeamus.

Ramadan, Abdel Azim (1993) "Fundamentalist Influence in Egypt: The Strategies of the Muslim Brotherhood and the Takfir Groups". In Martin E. Marty and R. Scott Appleby (eds) *Fundamentalisms and the State: Remaking Politics, Economics, and Militance*. Chicago: University of Chicago Press.

Rhein, Eberhard (1996) "Europe and the Mediterranean: A Newly Emerging Geopolitical Area?" *European Foreign Affairs Review*. Vol. 1, Issue 1.

Rheingold, Howard (1995) *The Virtual Community: Finding Connection in a Computerized World*. London: Minerva.

Riegel, Henrietta (1996) "Into the Heart of Irony: Ethnographic Exhibitions and the Politics of Difference". In Sharon Macdonald and Gordon Fyfe (eds) *Theorizing Museums: Representing Identity and Diversity in a Changing World*. Oxford: Blackwell Publishers & The Sociological Review.

Robins, Kevin (1995) "Cyberspace and the World We Live in". In Mike Featherstone and Roger Burrows (eds) *Cyberspace/Cyberbodies/Cyberpunk: Cultures of Technological Embodiment*. London, Thousand Oaks, New Delhi: Sage.

Rosen, Lawrence (1989) *The Anthropology of Justice: Law as Culture in Islamic Society*. Cambridge: Cambridge University Press.

Roy, Olivier (1994) (1992) *The Failure of Political Islam*. London: I.B. Tauris.

Sachs, Hiram (1995) "Computer Networks and the Formation of Public Opinion: An Ethnographic Study". *Media, Culture & Society*. Vol. 17, No. 1.

Sadiki, Larbi (1995) "Guided Democracy in Algeria and Egypt". *Australian Journal of International Affairs*. Vol. 49, No. 2.

Sanders, Åke (1997) "To What Extent is the Swedish Muslim Religious?" In Steven Vertovec and Ceri Peach (eds) *Islam in Europe: The Politics of Religion and Community.* London: MacMillan Press & New York: St. Martin Press.

Sayyid, Bobby (1994) "Sign O'Times: Kaffirs and Infidels Fighting the Ninth Crusade". In Ernesto Laclau (ed.) *The Making of Political Identities.* London & New York: Verso.

Scheff, Thomas (1994) "Emotions and Identity: A Theory of Ethnic Nationalism". In Craig Calhoun (ed.) *Social Theory and Politics of Identity.* Oxford: Blackwell.

Schulze, Reinhard (1991) "The Forgotten Honour of Islam". In Ami Ayalon (ed.) *Middle East Contemporary Survey.* Vol. XIII 1989. Boulder, San Francisco & Oxford: Westview Press.

Shepard, William E. (1996) "Muhammed Saʾid al-ʾAshmawi and the Application of the Shariʾa in Egypt". *International Journal of Middle East Studies.* Vol. 28. ss. 39–58.

Shukrallah, Hala (1994) "The Impact of the Islamic Movement in Egypt". *Feminist Review.* No. 47, Summer.

Singer, Hanaa Fikry (1993) *The Socialist Labor Party: A Case Study of a Contemporary Egyptian Opposition Party.* Cairo Papers in Social Science. Vol. 16, Monograph 1. Cairo: The American University in Cairo Press.

Steinberg, Gerald M. (1996) "The Arab–Israeli Security Dilemma and the Peace Process". *The International Security.* Vol. XXXI, No. 4, October–December.

Tiukkanen, Sari-Maarit (1994) "Islamilainen konferenssijärjestö O.I.C. poliittisena toimijana". In Tuomo Melasuo (ed.) *Vieras Välimeri. Kulttuurien ja politiikan kohtauspaikka.* Tutkimuksia, No. 59. Tampere: Tampereen Rauhan-ja konfliktintutkimuskeskus.

Tovias, Alfred (1996) "The EU's Mediterranean Policies Under Pressure". In Richard Gillespie (ed.) *Mediterranean Politics.* Vol. 2. London: Pinter.

Tölölyan, Khachig (1996) "Rethinking *Diaspora*(s): Stateless Power in the Transnational Moment". *Diaspora.* Vol. 5, No. 1.

Utvik, Bjørn Olav (1993) "Islamism: Digesting Modernity the Islamic Way". *Forum for Development Studies.* No. 2.

Waarderburg, Jacques (1978) "Official and Popular Religion in Islam". *Social Compass.* Vol. 25, No. 3–4.

Webman, Esther (1997) "Islamic Politics – Between Dialogue and Conflict". In Bruce Maddy-Weitzman (ed.) *Middle East Contemporary Survey*. Vol. XIX 1995. Boulder, San Francisco & Oxford: Westview Press.

Willis, Michael (1996) "The Islamist Movements of North Africa". In Roberto Aliboni, George Joffé and Tim Niblock (eds) *Security Challenges in the Mediterranean Region*. London: Frank Cass.

Väyrynen, Tarja (1997) "Kulttuurien törmäys: dialoginen etiikka konfliktien ratkaisemisen perustana". In Aini Linjakumpu (ed.) *Eurooppa tänään – 900 vuotta ristiretkien perintöä*. Tutkimustiedote, No. 72. Tampere: Tampereen Rauhan-ja konfliktintutkimuskeskus.

Youssef, Michael (1985) *Revolt against Modernity: Muslim Zealots and the West*. Leiden: E.J. Brill.

Zdanowski, Jerzy (1988) "The Society of the Muslim Brothers. A Study of Political Movement". *Studies on the Developing Countries*. No. 2.

Zubaida, Sami (1996) "Trajectories of Political Islam". *Index of Censorship*. No. 4.

Official documents

Agenda 2000. Communication of the Commission. DOC 97/6. Strasbourg, 15 July 1997.

Background note: "Intercultural Dialogue: A Basis for Co-operation": International colloquy in the framework of the Transmed Symposium of Civil Society. Malta, 12–14 April 1997.

Barcelona Declaration adopted at the Euro-Mediterranean Conference, 27–28 November 1995.

Conclusions. Second Euro-Mediterranean Ministerial Conference, Malta 15–16 April 1997. http://noel.diplomacy.edu/euromed/GETEX-TX.ASP?IDconv=2039.

Discours de Monsieur Habib Ben Yahia, Ministre des Affaires Etrangères de la République Tunisienne à la Conference Euro-Méditerranéenne. Barcelona, 27–28 November 1995. In unpublished publication: Partenariat Euro-Mediterraneen. Conférence euro-méditerranéenne de Barcelone (27–28 November 1995) – Discours des ministres. Euro-Med 2/95.

Euro-Mediterranean Partnership. Information note No 8. Cultural heritage. Internet-lähde: http://noel.diplomacy.edu/euromed/GETEXTX.ASP? IDconv=2030; 25 July 1997.

Intervention de Monsieur Mohamed Salah Dembri. Ministre des Affaires Etrangères à la Conférence Euro-Méditerranéenne. République Algérienne Démocratique et Populaire. In unpublished publication: Partenariat Euro-Mediterraneen. Conférence euro-méditerranéenne de Barcelone (27–28 November 1995) – Discours des ministres. Euro-Med 2/95.

On the Implementation of Financial and Technical Cooperation with the Mediterranean Non-member Countries and on Financial Cooperation with those as a Group. Commission of the European Communities: Report from the Commission to the Council and the European Parliament. COM(94) 384 final, Brussels, 18 November 1994, 16.

Progress report on the Euro-Mediterranean Partnership and preparations for the second conference of foreign affair ministers. Communication from the Commission to the Council and the European Parliament. COM(97) 68 final, Brussels, 19 February 1997.

Rede des Präsidenten des Europäischen Parlaments Dr. Klaus Hänsch. Eröffnungssitzung der Mittelmeerkonferenz am 27. November 1995 in Barcelona. In unpublished publication: Partenariat Euro-Mediterraneen. Conférence euro-méditerranéenne de Barcelone (27–28 November 1995) – Discours des ministres. Euro-Med 2/95.

Speech Minister van Mierlo voor de Barcelona-conferentie. In unpublished publication: Partenariat Euro-Mediterraneen. Conférence euro-méditerranéenne de Barcelone (27–28 November 1995) – Discours des ministres. Euro-Med 2/95.

Statement by Egypt. Minister of Foreign Affairs of the Egypt and the 2nd Euro-Mediterranean Conference in Malta. 15–16 April 1997.

Statement by Palestine Liberation Organization. Palestine National Authority, Office of President. The 2nd Euro-Mediterranean Conference in Malta. 15–16 April 199 (unofficial translation) www.diplomacy.edu/euromed/minist/speaches/palest.htm.

Statement by Syria (H. E. Mr Farouk al-Sharaʾ). Minister of Foreign Affairs of the Syrian Arab Republic at the 2nd Euro-Mediterranean Conference in Malta. 15–16 April 1997. www.diplomacy.edu/euromed/minist/speaches/syria.htm.

Statement by Turkey. Deniz Baykal: Deputy prime minister and foreign minister of the Republic of Turkey. Euro-Mediterranean Conference, Barcelona, 27 November 1995 (unpublished document).

Strengthening the Mediterranean Policy of the European Union: Establishing a Euro-Mediterranean Partnership. Commission of European Communities: Communication from Commission to the Council and the European Parliament. COM(94) 427 final, Brussels, 19 October 1994, 4.

Strengthening the Mediterranean Policy of the European Union: Proposals for Implementing a Euro-Mediterranean Partnership. Commission of the European Communities: Communication from the Commission to the Council and the European Parliament. COM(95) 72 final, Brussels, 8 March 1995, 18.

Documents by the Muslim Brotherhood

Mashhour, Mustafa (1995) "God is sufficient for us; the Best Guardian is He". In *Democracy in Crisis*. Published by Egyptian Action Group, London.

Muslim Brotherhood (1993) *Violence*. www.prelude.co.uk/prelude/mb/studies/violence.html; 4 May 1996.

Muslim Brotherhood (1995) *15 principles for agreement.*

Muslim Brotherhood (1995) *Our Testimony*. Copyrighted translation. Published by International Islamic Forum, London.

Muslim Brotherhood (n.d.) *Muslim Women in the Muslim Society.*

Muslim Brotherhood (n.d.) *A brief note in shura in Islam and the plurality of parties in Muslim society.*

Interviews (undertaken by Aini Linjakumpu)

Auer, Lawrence – Brussels, 16 December 1997

El-Helbawy, Kamal – London, 5 December 1997

El-Helbawy, Kamal – London, 18 December 1998

El-Hudaybi, Mahmud – Cairo, 22 February 1997

El-Hudaybi, Mahmud – Cairo, 3 March 1997

Huweidy, Fahmi – Cairo, 3 March 1997

Huweidy, Amira – Cairo, 17 February 1997

Khader, Bichara – Louvain-la-Nouve, 16 December 1997

Abu'lla Madi Abu'lla and Habib, Rafiq – Cairo, 3 March 1997

Index

A

Afganistan   113
Abu'lla, Abu'lla Madi   91
Algeria   27, 45, 60
American Muslim Council   144
Anderson, Benedict   18
Arab nationalism   48
Arkoun, Muhammed   111
ARPANET   98
articulation   14–18, 21, 24, 32, 35, 37,
    59, 67, 74–5, 78, 93, 101–3, 105–6,
    112, 114–15, 117–18, 122–3, 129,
    131, 135
    of Islam   35, 42, 44, 53–4, 56–7, 63, 68,
    78, 80, 84, 90, 92, 94, 129, 132, 147
Atatürk, Kemal   138
Ayubi, Aziz   9, 10
Al-Azhar   113

B

al-Banna, Hassan   60–1
Barcelona   27–8, 34, 132
Barcelona Conference   27, 29–30, 32, 34
Barcelona Declaration   29–30, 32–6,
    39–40, 42, 44–5
Ben Ali, president   138–9
Bologna   36
Butter, David   85

C

Cairo   113
Camp David agreement   87
Cannes   29
Claes, Willy   31
Common Foreign and Security Policy
    (CFSP)   30, 39, 41
computer–mediated communication
    (CMC)   97
Cyprus   27

D

dar-al-islam   20
Dejanews   99
diaspora   116–17, 122–3, 146

E

Egypt   27, 45, 49, 59–61, 63, 66, 68, 70,
    80–81, 90–1, 137, 139, 140–1
Eickelman, Dale   9
Elkins, David   116
Esposito, John   5, 8, 18, 106
Essen   29
Euro–Mediterranean Area   29
Euro–Mediterranean conference   27
Euro–Mediterranean Partnership
    Declaration   27
exclusion   140–1

F

Fandy, Mamoun   82, 86
Farouk I   61
fatwa   134, 135
15 principles for agreement   64, 68–9, 72,
    74–5, 78
Forum Civil Euro–Med   34, 37
France   19
Free Officers   61
fundamentalism   31–2, 139

G

Ghaddafi, Muhammed   112
global
    action   ix, 142
    communality   115, 142, 146
globalization   135–6, 147
    of Islam   131, 144, 147
Global Mediterranean Policy (GMP)
    29
Golden Era   112

Great Britain   98
Grossberg, Lawrence   15
Gulf War   11, 32

H
Habib, Rafiq   91
hadith   4–5, 9, 74, 77, 104, 106, 110
Ul-Haq, Zia   112
Hassner, Pierre   42
hate crime   143
El-Helbawy, Kamal   62, 77–9
Hobsbawn, Erik   107, 110
Holland   132
El-Hudaybi, Mahmud   64, 67, 69–71
Huntington, Samuel   17, 31
Hussein, Adel   82–3
Huweidy, Fahmi   50

I
identity   viii, 17, 19–20, 24, 31, 35,
    39–44, 54, 56–7, 59, 63, 71–3, 75–6,
    79–80, 84, 92–4, 97, 107, 110–11,
    115, 122–3, 137, 139, 146
ijma   5
imam   49
ijtihad   6
inclusion   141
Internet discussion groups   ix, 22, 97–9,
    101, 114, 117, 122, 130
Iran   60, 136–7
IRC community   146
Islam
    de-politicization of   90–92
    globalization of   131, 135–6
    interpretation of   3–5, 8, 77, 100–6,
        108, 110, 112–4
    monopolization of   47, 49–50
    'official'   60
    over-politicization of   viii, 6–10, 21
    politicization of   vii, ix, 11, 14, 22, 28,
        61–2, 71, 81, 85–6, 100–2
    politicizing   73, 84, 94, 107, 129–30
    privatization of   53
    subjectification of   102
    orthopraxian religion   106
Islamic
    Alliance   82–3
    community   56–7, 92, 103, 110, 117,
        121–4, 148

militancy   81
militants   86–90
Party   50
'threath'   140
Islamization   81, 83–4, 106–7, 110–11,
    138, 140
Islamism   51, 59–60, 85, 131, 136–142,
    147
    internationalizing   139
Israel   7, 27, 45, 116–17, 120–1, 132–4

J
al-Jama'a al-Islamia   87–9
Jerusalem   122, 133
al-Jihad   87
Joffé, George   36
Jordan   27

K
Karawan, Ibrahim   87, 90, 141
Khader, Bichara   46
Khomeini, Ayatollah   134
Krämer, Gudrun   73

L
Labor Party   81–6, 92
laïcite   92, 137
Lebanon   27, 45
Lévy, Pierre   99
Liberal Party   86
Libya   112
London   139

M
Malta   27, 34, 37, 132
Marks, Jon   47
Marxism   48
Mashour, Mustafa   69
McLuhan, Marshall   142
McNay, Lois   19
Mediterranean Co-operation   35
Middle East peace process   38, 132,
    134–6, 147
Morocco   27, 49
Mubarak, Hosni   85, 88
MUD community   146

N
Nasr, Muhammed Hamid Abul   69

National Democratic Party   66, 85
National Dialogue   85
Nasser, Abdel   61, 82
Neumann, Iver B.   40
New Mediterranean Policy   29
New Fafd Party   82, 86, 88

O
Organization of Islamic Conference (OIC)
    55–6, 130
Oslo Agreement   133

P
Pakistan   112
Palestine   7, 120–1
Palestinian Authority   7, 27, 45, 133
Peacenet   146
peace process *see* Middle East peace process
"Peoples of the Book"   119
Piscatori, James   9
Poland   40
politicization   viii, 18–19, 22, 101, 107,
    131, 134
    of Islam   vii, ix, 11, 14, 22, 28, 61–2,
    71, 81, 85–6, 100–2
Prophet Mohammed   4, 9, 18, 49, 69,
    74–5, 106, 108–11

Q
Qasim, TaPat Fu²ad   89
Quran   4, 74, 77–8, 103–4, 108, 110
Qutb, Sayed   87
qyias   5

R
Ramadan, Abdel Azim   67
Ranger, Terence   107, 110
Rhein, Eberhard   47
Riegel, Henrietta   36
Robins, Kevin   142
Roy, Oliver   138
Rushdie affair   134–6, 147
Rushdie, Salman   32, 134

S
Sachs, Hiram   146
Sadat, Anwar   61, 82, 87
Sadiki, Larbi   139
Schmid, Alex   48

secularism   137–8
secularization   92
sharia   5, 67–9, 70–3, 79, 84
Shia Islam   105
Shia Muslims   105
Shukrallah, Hala   73
Soviet Union   30–1
sunna   4–5
Sunni Islam   5, 112
Sunni Muslims   105
Syria   27, 132–3

T
Tagammu Party   85
Taleban   78, 106, 112
tawhid   8
territoriality   115
terrorism   7, 32, 43–8, 50, 52–7, 89–90
The Satanic Verses   134
Treaty of Rome   29
Tunisia   27, 49, 138–140
Turkey   27, 45, 50, 137

U
ulama   5, 112–4
United States of America   7, 30–1, 98,
    121, 132, 143, 145
umma   ix, 18, 20, 55, 97, 123–4

V
victimization   118
virtual community   122, 142
virtual *umma*   123–4

W
al-Wasat   81, 90–2
Welfare Party   138
Welsch, Jennifer M.   40
World War II   61
World Wide Web   98

Y
Young Egypt   81–2

Z
Zionism   120